SILK PAINTING
for Fashion and Fine Art

SILK PAINTING
for Fashion and Fine Art

Techniques for Making Ties, Scarves, Dresses, Decorative Pillows, and Fine Art Paintings

SUSAN LOUISE MOYER

Revised Edition

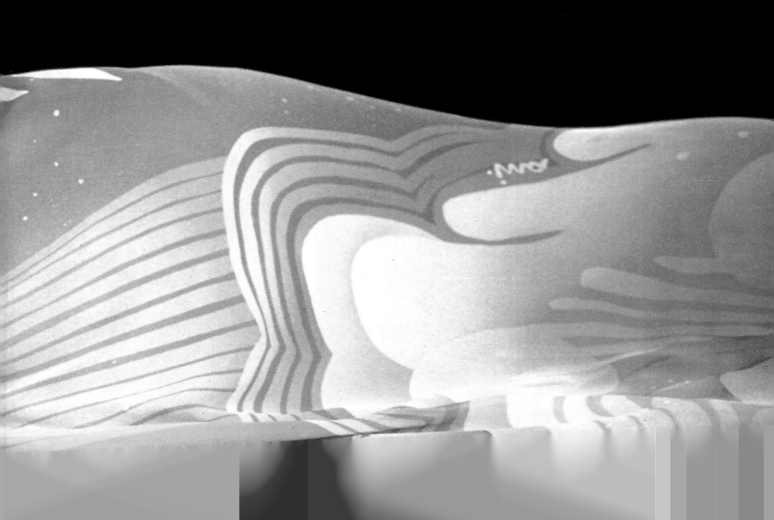

Front cover:
UNTITLED. © Susan Louise Moyer.

Page 1:
SCARF DRESS. © Susan Louise Moyer. Photo by Horizon Studios.

Page 2:
UNTITLED. © 1989 Ina Kozel.

Page 14:
FRINGE SCARF. © Susan Louise Moyer.

Page 80:
UNTITLED. © Susan Louise Moyer.

First Edition Edited by Alisa Palazzo
Revised Edition Edited by Susan Preston
Designed by Dale E. Moyer
Graphic production by Ellen Greene / Dale E. Moyer

Copyright © 2004 Susan Louise Moyer
First published in 1995 in the United States by Watson-Guptill Publications.
Revised edition published in 2004 in the United States by Moyer Design, Inc.,
PO Box 2875, Fort Bragg, CA 95437-2875.

Library of Congress Cataloging-in-Publication Data

Moyer, Susan Louise.
    Silk painting for fashion and fine art: techniques for making ties, scarves,
dresses, decorative pillows, and fine art paintings / Susan L. Moyer.
        p.   cm.
    Includes index.
    ISBN 0-9725695-0-2 (pbk.) (previously published by Watson-Guptill
Publications, ISBN 0–8230–4831–4)
    1. Silk painting. 2. Textile painting. I. Title.
TT851.M69 1995
746.6 — dc20   95–22731
                                                            CIP

Printed in Malaysia

First printing, 1995

First Printing, Revised Edition, 2004

1 2 3 4 5 6 / 08 07 06 05 04

TO SARAH LOUISE AND HEIDI JEANNE

Acknowledgments

My deepest appreciation goes to the artists whose silk creations are included in this book, many of whom have participated in my workshops: Len Brondum, Elaine Gima, Elizabeth Heber, Ellen Tobey-Holmes, Suzanne Perilman, Jeanette Shires, and Merridee Joan Smith. It gives me great pleasure to see these artists working with the techniques and inspiration that they have gleaned from the world of surface design to develop their own artistic voice. I would also like to thank Karen Rosen and Carole Mondress of Kalalani Silk, Bunny Bowen, Vello Laanaemaa, and Kai Vaarandi for giving me the opportunity to include their wonderful silk creations in this revised edition of *Silk Painting for Fashion and Fine Art.* Thanks to all the students who have participated in my workshops for their enthusiasm and insightful questions that help me define the needs of my readers, and to my colleague Betsy Sterling Benjamin for her expertise regarding chapter 7. Additional thanks to Jeanette Shires for keeping the office of Moyer Design and Silk Painting going smoothly while I revised several chapters, to Michael Katz and Kim Meyer for their technical support in chapter 1, to Anna Bernhard for her gracious cooperation in procuring Elaine Gima's art. And I wish to express a warm thank you to Maurice and Yvette Bendahan, for their friendship and support regarding the business of publishing.

And finally, a special thanks to my husband, Dale, who encouraged me to revise and republish *Silk Painting for Fashion and Fine Art,* for his beautiful book design and photography, and for his devotion and friendship. And a very special thank you to Sarah Louise Moyer and Heidi Jeanne Reddig who keep me smiling.

CONTENTS

FANTASY FISH © Jeanette Shires.

Dress. © 1990 Ina Kozel

INTRODUCTION

There are many expressive and beautiful objects of art that incorporate handpainted silk. Whether for home decor and fashion or fine art, these different applications require specific materials, techniques, and design considerations.

In my previous book, *Silk Painting: The Artist's Guide to Gutta and Wax Resist Techniques,* I introduced readers to the basic tools, procedures, and enjoyment of silk painting, enabling them to become skilled at, and sensitive to, their craft. In this book, I strive to expand on those techniques and to address how one can embellish the more traditional uses of silk and build ideas for more elaborate projects. I recommend that you read this entire book through first so that when you begin a project, whether it be a painting or a fashion accessory, you can establish the proper foundation to bring your work to successful completion. And, for the readers who are just venturing into silk painting, I suggest that they first practice the methods demonstrated in chapter 6 (Linear Underpainting and Layering Techniques).

My wish is to expose you to the various applications, techniques, and materials available and inspire you to set new, exciting goals. By suggesting flexible guidelines, not absolutes, I endeavor to engage the reader in a dialogue between the technical foundation and creative considerations; therefore, when the reader reaches a goal, the solutions are truly a reflection of his own creative growth. On the following pages, the examples of artistic expression show how completely unique silk painting allows you to be.

As a silk painter, I have a strong commitment to establishing silk painting as a respected, creative art medium, not merely a craft that will soon fade out of fashion. Only through serious effort will silk painting gain the respect it deserves. It has the ability to evolve along with us and reflect the endless potential of our creativity. Just as a medium should not inhibit our creative potential, the evolution of that medium should not in turn be stifled by our lack of commitment to it as an expressive vehicle.

Founded in 1977, the Surface Design Association has championed the art of silk painting and has been a great source of inspiration and knowledge for me and many of the professional artists represented in this book. Another well-established organization is the American Craft Council, which was founded in 1943 and is affiliated with the Museum of Art & Design, New York City. These organizations have established high standards of professionalism among artists and promote the appreciation of their work by the public. They educate, impart information, and inspire us to greater artistic heights, and their efforts should be acknowledged.

It is my hope that this book might in some way also inspire you to explore your own creative potential and to share your knowledge and enthusiasm with the rest of the growing silk painting community.

GONDOLAS, VENICE. © 1993 Natashe Foucault

Eclipse (screen). © 1992 Betsy Sterling Benjamin

BROADWAY. © Susan L. Moyer

HORSE. (Silk-wrapped papier-mâché). © Judith Bateman and Suzanne Bateman-Smith

THIN VEIL. © Susan L. Moyer

LUNAR BEACH. © Susan L. Moyer

PART ONE: Basic Concepts

Any fine artist must have a good foundation prior to embarking on more advanced methods of creative expression. Here you will find the essential information on tools, color theory, design and layout, and basic fashion projects. Silk painting is a gratifying and aesthetically beautiful means of artistic expression. But it can be even more exciting and rewarding when your creations are useful items that enhance your daily life. With these techniques in hand, you can create fashion garments and home furnishings, as well as fine silk paintings. Each time you prop yourself up on the couch with that painted silk pillow, or don that elegant silk scarf for the finishing touch to an outfit, you will be experiencing your art, instead of simply looking at it.

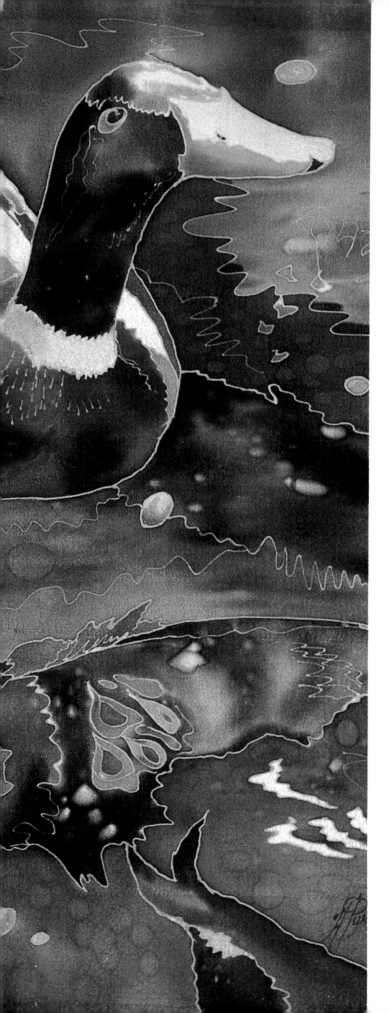

1 MATERIALS AND TOOLS

For 4,000 years, silk has been prized as a beautiful and luxurious fabric, at once stylish and practical. And for as long as this versatile and enticing fiber has been valued, it has also been decorated. Silk painting procedures have been passed down through centuries of development and from many countries, including India, Russia, and China, and they are still evolving today. This diverse medium naturally lends itself to a variety of projects and techniques, all requiring different tools and processes.

Whether creating a functional scarf or tie, or a decorative pillow or wall-hanging, silk painters, like all artists, must understand their materials: the dyes, diluents, resists, brushes, and, of course, the silks themselves. Armed with these tools and with an appreciation and respect for the medium, you will be ready to explore the exciting uses and creative potential of silk.

DUCK AND FISH. © 1992. Natashe Foucault

SILKS AND THEIR CARE

Silk, a natural fiber, has many applications for the silk painter. The fabric brings luster and depth to the color, and the drape of many weaves is flowing and sensuous. In order, to determine the suitability of silk for a specific project, it is important for the silk painter to know the limitations, as well as the attributes, of the fiber and various weaves with relation to intended techniques and applications.

Silk fabrics are measured in units called mommes (mm), with 5 to 10 mommes being relatively lightweight and 12 mommes and up being more medium weight and durable. Silk fibers are easily dyed, but the different textures and weights of the various fabrics will affect dye flow, drying time, and color saturation. Dye will flow freely on a 14mm crepe (which is stretchy and durable) or a 10mm habutai (a fairly delicate, lightweight plain-weave silk) because the threads of these fabrics are tightly woven, enhancing capillary action. The dye will flow less easily on loose or open weaves like chiffon, because the fibers are farther apart.

You should also keep the fabric weight in mind when choosing a resist. Gutta resist, for example, can be thinned to penetrate the smooth surface of a 19.5mm silk charmeuse without difficulty. But, it will not penetrate and seal most textured or nubby weaves or heavy fabrics. Hot wax, on the other hand, will easily penetrate and create a resist on the more textured and medium weight silks.

For a small fee, many suppliers make swatch sets of the various silks they carry. As a point of reference, the swatches are well worth the investment. You can test your dyes and resists on them before making a major fabric purchase, as well as pick and choose from among the varieties of silk weaves and weights.

As a fashion fabric, the weaves and weights of the different textures will affect the flow and line of the garment and the durability of home furnishings. Silk, when dye painted is fairly wrinkle resistant, absorbent, comfortable, cool in the summer, and warm in the winter. Most silks are washable and resistant to mildew and moths, if cleaned and stored properly. On the other hand, silk fibers are weakened by perspiration, antiperspirant, and chlorine bleach. Silk used for draperies and home decor will also deteriorate rapidly if exposed to the sunlight, so treat your silk artwork like fine watercolor paintings or pastel drawings and keep them out of direct light. When stored, silk fabric should not be kept in airtight plastic containers or bags, but rather wrapped in acid-free tissue paper and placed in a cardboard box or cloth garment bag so the silk can breathe.

Silk paintings can be washed in a nonalkaline detergent, as long as the dyes are set properly. A garment that is made with yards of fabric or is intricately constructed, however, should be dry cleaned to maintain its shape. In some cases, delicately constructed garments should be spot cleaned. Note that dry cleaning solvents such as perchloroethylene do not contain water, which may cause fibers to swell and shrink, and dyes to bleed.

Preparing Silk for Painting

Preparing the silk properly is crucial to the success of your project. Fiber-art suppliers recommend that you prewash silk prior to starting a project, in order to remove any dirt spots or sizing that might effect the even application of color and resist. Depending upon the layout and design of your project, it may be prudent to preshrink the fabric. In this way, you will avoid having your painting or garment layout shrink during steam fixation. You can use lukewarm water and Synthrapol, a nonionic concentrated liquid detergent sold by many fiber-art suppliers. This product will also

These are sample swatches of various types of silk. Available from most fabric suppliers, they are useful for choosing the appropriate fabric and testing dye and resist prior to purchasing your silk and beginning a project.

remove most fabric sizing that may impede dye penetration. Soak the silk in warm water for an hour, then rinse and wash in Synthrapol. Rinse several times to remove all chemicals. If you use a washing machine, periodically check the silk to be sure it has not become twisted and permanently wrinkled.

As an alternative to prewashing scarf blanks, I first stretch the silk onto my Moyer Design Fabric Stretching System (see pages 28, 29). If I then see spots or dull areas on the surface, I wet the entire surface with a sponge brush and alcohol diluent. I then go back and lightly rub the spotted area in question with the brush to dissolve any dirt. To dry the stretched silk I use a hair dryer which shrinks the fabric and also eliminates wrinkles and the need to iron.

You can also stretch silk using light weight canvas stretcher bars and tacks. Embroidery hoops can be used for testing colors and small items. One type is plastic with a pliable rubber hoop that will not snag the silk. Another option for stretching small work, executed with solvent based resists, is to iron your silk to the plastic side of heavy freezer paper. The solvent dissolves the plastic, creating a seal and thus a barrier that prevents the dye from traveling. Even though this method may require a few adjustments to your technique, it beats lugging frames when teaching crafters or when plein air painting.

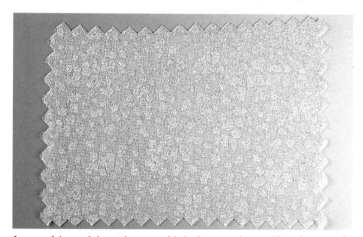

Jacquard is an elaborately woven fabric that contains motifs and textures in its weave. These patterns can add depth and interest to a design.

Pongee is a tightly woven, plain silk. It receives dye well and is durable and available in both medium and heavy weights. After it is steamed and dry-cleaned, pongee becomes much softer, and its luster improves with wear.

A luxurious surface to paint on, crepe de chine *is the smoothest and most lustrous of all the crepe fabrics. It is durable and resilient and accepts the dye evenly. The elasticity of the weave gives crepe de chine a beautiful drape, making it a good silk for garments.*

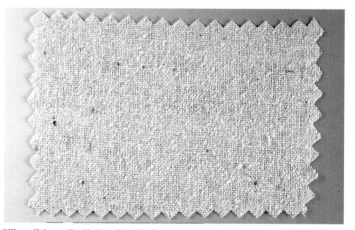

Silk noil is easily distinguishable from other silks by its natural off-white color, nubby flecks, and rough texture. This texture is caused by pieces of the silkworm cocoon, which remain in the fibers through the harvesting and weaving processes. Dye does not flow easily on silk noil, and the fabric is not as durable as some others because its fibers are very short.

Charmeuse has the smoothest, most lustrous finish of all the silks. It comes in a variety of weights and is fairly durable, but it should still be handled with care because the finish can be easily marred. Different types of charmeuse, such as crepe-back and satin-back charmeuse, are distinguished by the weave on the reverse side of the fabric. The sheen of this silk gives added brilliance to dye colors.

DYES AND DILUENTS

The liquid dyes that work with the silk painting techniques presented in this book are mostly from the acid group of dyes. To fix (or permanently set) them in the fabric once a garment or painting is finished, and to develop their full color, acid dyes need saturated steam (see chapter 9, page 130, steam fixation). The fiber-reactive family, another type of dye used in silk painting, is explored in chapter 8, Screen Printing. These dyes come in both powder and liquid form and, unlike acid dyes, must be activated with manufacturer-recommended chemicals. They also usually require steam fixing for setting.

Several manufacturers make liquid silk dyes: Pébéo (Pébéo Soie is their line of silk-fabric dyes), H. Dupont, and Sennelier (Tinfix Design), all manufactured in France. All of these are considered acid dyes (requiring steam fixing) and can therefore be mixed and used together.

Another brand of liquid dye is Jacquard, which is also available in the United States. Jacquard Red Label and Green Label Silk Colors are modified fiber-reactive dyes that differ slightly in behavior and chemistry from acid dyes mentioned above; therefore, the manufacturer does not recommend mixing or blending them with other brands. The Red Label dyes require steam fixing. The Green Label dyes can be fixed by steam or in a chemical bath made from water and a dye-setting concentrate. The chemical bath method limits their compatibility with many wax resist and layering techniques, because the wax that is used to cover (and save) certain layers of dyes may retard the chemical bath, preventing it from fixing those colors. On the other hand, if you use the Green Label dyes along with Jacquard's water-soluble-resist, the dye-setting bath will wash away this resist, thus eliminating steam setting and dry cleaning (which would otherwise be required to remove a rubber-based resist). This makes the Green Label Silk dyes particularly easy to use. Art instructors also appreciate the simplicity of process the Green Label dyes provide when working with children in the classroom.

Silk painters working with the Jacquard dyes often find it helpful to use a small amount of Jacquard No-Flow. Also called anti-diffusant or epaississant, this clear liquid is brushed directly onto the silk prior to painting or is added directly to the dyes. It helps to control the flow while you are blending and shading colors, and allows for the buildup of textural effects. When using the Green Label colors, make sure they are bone dry before submerging them in the dye-setting solution by going over them with a warm hair drier (even if the fabric feels dry to the touch). Since silk naturally holds moisture, if you don't take this precaution, when your painting is placed in the setting solution the dye may wash out.

With extended exposure to both indoor and outdoor light, some dye colors will fade. When the artwork will be exposed to light and longevity is important, you might consider working with flowing paints such as Pébéo/Setasilk, Sennelier/Silkcolor or Jacquard Dye-na-flow. These products have been formulated for painting on silk and are heat set with an iron. Since they are pigments bound with acrylic, they leave a slight hand on the silk but are refined enough to allow the sheen and texture of the silk to reveal itself. The slight hand is not an issue if the silk application is wall art, art quilts or home furnishings. Plus these are applications that are exposed to much more light over time than wearables which live much of their lives stored in a closet.

When working with the flowing paints, as the colors start to dry they grab the silk quickly, making blending difficult. The key to success is to keep the working surface wet. Kai Vaarandi and Vello Laanemaa, who work with Setasilk, partially immerse a large absorbent sponge or piece of foam rubber in a shallow pan of water under their stretched silk. The water evaporating off the exposed surface of the sponge rises, thus keeping the stretched silk above wet. In some cases you can keep your work in progress wet by spraying the surface with a fine mist of water.

Manufacturers of acid dyes recommend adding 10 percent diluent (either their own concentrated brand and water or your own alcohol and water mixture) to all colors, and more to obtain lighter tints, black being the exception. To obtain a rich, even black, do not dilute; instead, liberally apply one coat to the fabric at full strength. When the fabric is steamed, the black will become richer and darker. When overpainting (layering acid dyes one over another) with black dye on the more highly concentrated colors like yellow, the black often bleeds past the resist during steam fixation. This happens because black dye takes longer to strike (or set in) the fabric, so it continues to migrate looking for a place to strick after the colors have already saturated the fibers. To avoid migration, liberally dilute colors, especially when planning to overpaint them with black.

Tip for Steam Setting Acid Dyes

- To cut the steam fixation time in half and to eliminate most of the dye runoff after steaming, treat your silk with a light coat of Gojiru before painting (see page 99).

To mix pastel colors and tints, you must dilute the dyes. The diluent's job is not only to lighten your colors but to promote the even flow and application of dye. Most acid-dye manufacturers produce an alcohol-free, concentrated diluent that you mix with distilled water before adding to dye. The recommended proportions of diluent and water vary according to the manufacturer and are included in the packaging instructions. I recommend using the manufacturer's diluent with the water soluble and acrylic resists because it is not as corrosive to the resist as the alcohol diluents. When working with a stronger resist like rubber-based gutta or paraffin and beeswax, the dyes can also be diluted using a solution of isopropyl alcohol and distilled water at the following proportions:

- For alcohol with a 70-percent alcohol content, use ⅔-¾ alcohol to ⅓-¼ distilled water. Use less alcohol for blending tints on silk.

- For a brand with closer to a 90-percent alcohol content, use ½ alcohol to ½ distilled water (adjust for tints).

- To avoid isopropyl alcohol fumes, you can resort to Vodka "straight up."

When using isopropyl alcohol, it is advisable to wear rubber gloves and a face mask, and work in a well-ventilated space; the fumes are toxic, and the liquid is also highly flammable.

You can often avoid streaking and improve dye movement on the fabric ("wetting out" of fibers) not only by mixing the dyes with the manufacturer's diluent but by adding a touch of nonionic soap such as Ivory Liquid, Liquid Tide, or Synthrapol when diluting a color.

The different mixtures of diluents have various characteristics that work to help control your application of dye. Diluent that

Colors from a variety of sources. Steam set dye: Pébéo Soie, Sennelier (Tinfix Design), H. Dupont, and Jacquard. Iron (heat) set flowing paints: Dye-na-Flow, Setasilk, and Silkcolor.

contains alcohol keeps the dye in solution longer and dries faster on the silk. Manufacturers' diluents, mixed only with water will dry more slowly. A slower drying time will provide the opportunity to blend, shade, and manipulate the dye to create special effects, especially in a large area like a background. To get the benefit of a faster drying time and a more even flow of the dye, add the concentrated manufacturer's diluent to the alcohol and water diluent according to their instructions.

After the dye is on the silk, many textural effects are achieved by moving the dye with salt, alcohol diluent or water. This will work only when the dye has not started to strick (set in) the fabric and can still be dislodged and moved. Some colors strike more quickly then others, most notably the more brilliant hues, such as bright blues and hot pinks. Also, some of the mixed colors may separate when applied to the silk. These colors will be easier to work with when applying to broad, flat areas and around motifs, after alcohol, water and manufacturer's diluent have been added. Remember, too, that once you become familiar with the characteristics of different colors and their mixtures, you can use their seemingly difficult behavior to work for you in creating various nuances and special effects.

Use the manufacturer's diluents and soaps only once and not again when overpainting because hygroscopic ingredients (those that hold in moisture) added to dyes to promote fixing during the steaming process, as well as heavy salt residue left from salt techniques, may cause silk to retain a lot of moisture during the steaming process. If the fabric becomes too damp during steaming,

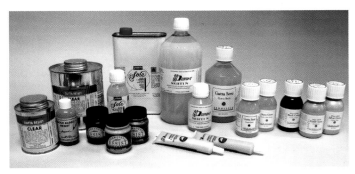

The various resists pictured here include clear gutta, water-soluble resists, acrylic black, and metallic resists manufactured by Rupert, Gibbon & Spider, Inc. (Jacquard), Pébéo, H. Dupont, and Sennelier.

the dye may migrate and the manufacturer's diluent or any detergent used may continue to act as a leveling agent, softening textural effects.

If stored in a dark cool place, acid dyes and the modified fiber reactive dyes are very stable and will last for years without losing their color. Although most manufacturers add a preservative to retard spoilage, once you add diluent, leftover dye should be labeled and dated. Although rare, some additives (other than alcohol) may cause the dye to spoil.

RESISTS

The primary job of a resist is to control the movement of dye by delineating and separating areas of color. Gutta and similar resists are most commonly applied to silk in a linear fashion with the use of an applicator. They can also be applied by the process of screen printing (see chapter 8). The resulting resist lines penetrate and seal the silk fibers, creating a barrier to contain the liquid dye and prevent it from flowing past the resist.

Each type of resist has specific qualities, which should be noted so that you use the proper one for a particular project. There are primarily three types of linear resists used in silk painting: the rubber-based (solvent) gutta resists, which come in clear, decorative, black and metallic; clear, water-soluble resists and pigmented decorative acrylic resists which come in a variety of colors and metallic.

Some decorative acrylic resists will withstand dry cleaning. Check the product label. On the other hand, metallic gutta and colored gutta will not withstand dry cleaning. Wax and clear gutta can be use in the same project to execute various techniques and textures and need to be completely removed from the fabric by dry cleaning.

Note: Check labels carefully. Gutta has become a generic term for other types of resists. Genuine gutta is rubber based, thinned with solvent and can be removed by dry cleaning. Acrylics (decorative resists) that are thinned with water are no longer water soluable once they have dried. Water-soluble resists are designed to be removed from the fabric and should wash out with water.

Clear Gutta

True gutta is a refined latex product dissolved in a solvent and is the resist preferred by many artists. They find that the rubbery gutta resist line will hold up to various techniques, which require repeated applications of dye, diluent, and alcohol. Clear gutta doesn't necessarily need to be thoroughly dry before painting but it does need some time to penetrate and seal the silk.

Once a painting has been finished and the dyes steam-set, clear gutta is removed from the silk by dry-cleaning. Because the dyes used in silk painting are not soluble in dry-cleaning fluids, it is also possible to remove the gutta before the dyes have been steam-set without disturbing the underlying color. Although it is preferable to dry-clean after the dyes are set, there may be times when you will want to remove the gutta or wax (explored in chapter 7) before proceeding with a painting.

Gutta is thinned to a working consistency with a solvent. The common solvents used are mineral spirits, naphtha, or solvents marketed by gutta manufacturers. For safety, wear latex gloves when handling the solvents, and store these flammable and toxic liquids in their original containers, which are specially made to keep the solvent from dissipating, or in a metal container.

CELEBRATION OF THE SEA. © Evelyn Jenkins Drew. *Executed with Jacquard dyes, this silk painting illustrates how a white outline (achieved by using a clear gutta) can be beautifully integrated as a design element.*

CUMULUS BEGONIA. © Evelyn Jenkins Drew. *This painting is an exquisite example of the incorporation of a colored resist as an integral part of the design, especially in the linear areas of the clouds and the pier.*

Some metal solvent containers found in art supply stores, like the one pictured on page 27 have a long spout, similar to that on an oil can. The tip twists open and closed and provides a very convenient way of adding the solvent to a gutta applicator.

Decorative Acrylic Resists

Decorative resists come in several colors, including black. According to the manufacturers, these heat set resists are water-based acrylics with pigments. I find they are more compatible with the hand of the silk when applied to plain woven 12mm and 14mm weight silks. Since the heavier weight fabrics have more fibers for the resist to bind with, the silk holds up better to the hand of the decorative resist. When working on light-weight silks (5mm or 8mm), the hand of the resist tends to be heavier than the silk, overpowering the beauty and feel of the silk. Also, the resist on lightweight or stretchy fabric has a tendency to ripple when the silk is released from the tension of the stretcher.

Many fiber artists use colored resist as a decorative element. If the decorative touches are applied before steaming, the resist will set during the steaming process. If the resist is applied after steaming, follow the manufacturers directions for heat setting.

Tips for Working with a Decorative Resist

- Do not store or ship decorative resists in hot or freezing conditions.
- If the resist comes in a bottle, shake the container well before pouring the contents into your applicator.
- If your resist is too thick, add water a little at a time. If the resist is too thin, stir and shake the container again.
- If the resist comes in a tube and has gotten thick, empty the resist into a resist applicator and add water.
- For a better seal, allow the resist to dry naturally without the use of a hair drier. For heavyweight fabrics, you may need to apply the resist to both sides of the silk. You can seal the back by applying a clear gutta, as long as the painting is only viewed from the front side.
- When steam setting, be sure to put a clean cloth (cotton or cotton polyester) next to your silk rather than steam-ing paper since the steaming paper may stick to the resist and ruin your work. The cloth can be washed and reused.
- Use a pressing cloth when ironing, to keep the resist from sticking to your iron and to avoid backstaining the silk.

CACTUS. © Linda France Hartge and David Hartge. *Linda uses black gutta not only as a linear resist, but also as a means of delineating form and creating textures in her paintings. She often uses black and clear guttas in the same painting.*

Decorative Metallic Resists

Metallic resists are available in both gutta and acrylic fabric-paint forms. Unlike clear gutta and water soluble resists, the decorative gutta and acrylic resists are meant to remain in the silk. The metallic gutta is not dry-cleanable, however, and over time will flake or rub off the silk. Unfortunately, fabric-paint resists, which are more durable, do not always penetrate and seal the medium weight silks causing the inevitable leaks. (see tips pages 25, 22)

A true metallic gold or silver resist that is durable, washable, dry-cleanable, and suitable for wearable art is a product many silk painters have been asking for. If you plan to work with gold or silver metallic resist, you might first find the chemist inside you and proceed with the determination to be master of your own materials. You will not be alone. Many fine and decorative artists like Ute Patel-Missfeldt, maintain quality control when working with certain pigments by compounding their own ingredients, such as oil paints, pastels, and gilding materials.

I met Ute Patel-Missfeldt at Galerie Smend in Cologne. She is a popular German silk painting teacher and artist, and the author of several books on the subject. Ute shared with me her method for making a very effective gold metallic resist. She adds a small amount of very fine gold metallic gilding powder (Kreul Bronze powder, 127620 Dunkelgold, which is available in the U.S.) to a decorative acrylic resist called Javana Lining Paint. This decorative acrylic resist comes in several colors, which, surprisingly, all become metallic gold when the gold powder is added, so any color you choose should work. Ute brings her resist to a working consistency by mixing in a few drops of water. The mixture is stable for about two hours, so she mixes only a little at a time.

Ute applies the acrylic metallic resist using a resist applicator or a special liner pen that she has designed and developed (page 25). The liner pen, which is an adaptation of an old-fashioned ruling pen, permits very even and controlled lines and curves. It is not, however, designed for fluid, freehand drawing. Mixing the resist to a consistency that is compatible with the liner pen takes some skill, but with practice it should become easier.

Even though many metallic acrylic resists are marketed as dry-clean-resistant, experience has taught me that they maybe washable and durable but not always dry-cleanable. I found the problem is not that the resist dissolves in the dry cleaning fluid but that metallic will rub off as the silk is tumbled against other fabrics during the cleaning process.

I was able to make metallic gold and silver gutta by adding a little Cres-Lite Bronze Powder (#601 for gold and #242 for silver) to a good-quality gutta. Cres-Lite is manufactured by Crescent Bronze Powder Company, Inc. Metallic powders come in a large selection of colors and grades of refinement; the coarser grades give more sparkle to the gutta, while the finer grades bind better with the gutta and maintain better resistance to flaking off. This homemade metallic gutta mixture is most effective if used within the first day or two, because fresh resist enables you to maintain a thin, even application on the silk, and it won't separate and flake off as easily as some of the commercial products. As with all decorative resists, metallic gutta can be more effective when applied to a plain weave versus a stretchy fabric.

If you are tempted to make your own metallic resist, acrylic mediums as well as the decorative acrylic resists that are currently on the market maybe worth exploring.

A note of caution:, remember that metallic bronzing powders are made from finely ground metals such as copper and aluminum, which you should avoid inhaling. Wear rubber gloves and a mask. Also, in order to keep the lite powder from becoming airborne, work in a an area that is free of drafts.

Water-Soluble Resist

Water-soluble resists are usually made from a variety of starch and gum thickeners. Water is used to thin them to a working consistency. These resists are a cousin to the rice paste resists used for centuries in China and Japan. They are washed out of the silk with water after the flowing paint has been heat set or the dye has been steam-set.

Many professional silk painters find that water-soluble resists limit the versatility of the medium, since they cannot endure the rigors of more complex painterly techniques. This is especially

BUTTERFLIES AND THISTLE. © Ellen Shannon. *A charming and stylized image, this piece was executed with gold metallic gutta, which greatly enhances the design.*

true when applying more than one application of dye. Here, the dye will ultimately break down a water-soluble resist. To help maintain the water-soluble resist from breaking down when painting, avoid flooding the silk with dye, and do not use alcohol diluent. To achieve a light colored resist line, liquid dye can be added to most water-soluble resists. The dye sets in the silk during the steam fixation process. Then, with care not to backstain the silk, the resist and any loose color is washed away.

When water-soluble resists are applied to a painted ground, they will discharge the dye, creating a lighter line of color on the ground. This happens because they contain water and other liquids that disturb the unset dye. Although some find this a problem, other artists integrate this characteristic into their design.

Some water-soluble resists need hot water and scrubbing to be removed from the silk, and during this process the painting may lose some color and the silk may become bruised . Also, some water-soluble resists become stiff and permanent when immersed in dry-cleaning fluids, or gummy when put in dye-setting solutions. So, always be sure that your water-soluble resist is compatible with the other processes you are planning to use.

Tip for Working with all Resists

• To avoid leaks when working with decorative resists or when you have drawn a narrow and thus delicate resist (gutta) line, add a touch of dye thickener to your color. Adjust the consistency so that the dye still flows freely off the brush and on the silk. The addition of dye thickener will impede the capillary action of the dye just enough to control the leaking.

RESIST APPLICATORS

Resist applicators are small, soft plastic squeeze bottles with metal tips available in various sizes. They offer the control needed to apply thin, even resist lines. Some metal tips have been threaded so that they will screw onto the cap of the applicator. There are two versions of this model; in one, the top screws onto the bottle, and in the other the top snaps into the bottle. The snap-in top has a slight tendency to pop out when the resist is being applied. To avoid this, cut off the very top end of the extra opaque hard plastic cap that comes with the applicator (pictured on page 27) and screw the altered cap over the snap-in top onto the applicator.

Other models may need to be assembled by pushing the metal tip up through the end of the applicator from the inside of the cap. To facilitate this, you will need to snip off the end of the small plastic tip. When a filled resist applicator is not in use, prevent the metal tip from clogging by inserted a pin in the tip. If a pin is not supplied with the applicator, use a silk pin, quilter's pin, beading needle or wire of the appropriate size for the purpose. To keep track of these tiny pins and their sizes, make a red label and attach it to the pin.

As you are applying the resist, the edges of the metal tips may drag slightly on the silk. This is not a terrible problem but you should know that one can round off the tip with a jeweler's file or any fine metal file so that the tip glides easily over the silk. With less resistance you will have more control of your resist drawing and application.

This photograph shows the reservoir of the liner pen developed by Ute Patel-Missfeldt being filled with a gold resist. The instrument is specially designed to provide an even, controlled line width when applying both straight and curved stylized lines. From the book Ute Patel-Missfeldt: Meisterschule Seidenmalerei *(Master School of Silk Painting), Augustus Verlag, 1993, Augsburg, Germany.*

A straight-edged ruler is used here as a guide when drawing lines with the liner pen. Tip: To keep the resist from smearing under the straight edge as you draw, suspend the edge above the surface of the silk by taping two coins to the underside of the ruler. Photo from the book Ute Patel-Missfeldt: Meisterschule Seidenmalerei *(Master School of Silk Painting), Augustus Verlag, 1993, Augsburg, Germany.*

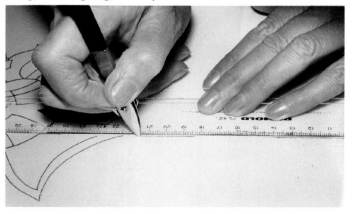

HARLEKIN. © Ute Patel-Missfeldt. Model: Isabel Patel. *In this painted silk cape-like jacket, Ute's design and use of gold shows the strong influences of both Art Nouveau and the culture of India on her work. She uses metallic resist as a strong design element in many of her projects. From the book* Seidenmonde mit Phantasie, *Eulen Verlag.*

HARLEKIN (detail). © Ute Patel-Missfeldt *To achieve the durable, metallic resist required for wearable art, Ute mixes metallic powders with liner paints.*

While most resists are packaged in large containers and should be transferred to a resist applicator for use, there are several water-based resists that come in tubes equipped with applicator tips; they can be applied directly onto the silk from the tube. They can also be emptied into the traditional, smaller applicator, which, as with all water-based resists, makes it possible to add water and adjust the consistency for application.

Also available is the Silkpaint Air Pen. It is a resist applicator with an electric air pump. You activate and control the flow of the resist by placing an index finger over the opening. The Air Pen was developed for silk painters with arthritic hands and carpal tunnel syndrome, who find it painful to squeeze resist through a plastic applicator. It is also a tool to help production artists avoid carpal tunnel syndrome. You can get small, medium, and large tips that fit the pen and enable the creation of medium- to heavy-weight resist lines. Although the pen is difficult to clean if you are using solvent-based resist, it is a very useful line applicator for a variety of water-based and water-soluble mediums. These products are easier to clean and flush out of the pen.

Filling the Resist Applicator

To fill the basic soft plastic applicator, hold it upright and squeeze in the sides. Hold the open gutta container 2 to 3 inches above the applicator. Pour the resist in a thin stream into the applicator until it is full. As you are pouring, if the resist begins to clog the opening, create a vacuum by releasing the pressure you are applying to the applicator sides. The resist will be pulled into the applicator and you can then continue pouring without the resist spilling over the top. A small funnel or squeeze top can also be a handy way to pour gutta but then you are left with something to clean (with solvent) before you can use it again. When working with gutta I try to keep my applicator full. If you are working in a humid environment, the wet air that is sucked into the applicator as it empties mixes with the gutta and tends to cause bubbles, uneven application and leaks in your gutta line.

Cleaning and Storing Resist Applicators

For ease of cleaning and storing it is advisable to have a resist applicator for each type and color resist you are working with. Gutta should never be left in the applicator for more than one or two days. The solvent in the gutta will dissipate through the porous plastic, leaving the gutta in a hardened state. To avoid this, either store a gutta-filled applicator in a tightly capped jar of solvent, or transfer the gutta back into its original container. After removing the gutta, lean the gutta applicator open side down against the inside of a small jar or disposable cup to air-dry for a day or more. Once the applicator is completely dry, clean the film of gutta from the inside with a cotton swab, twisting it until you have pulled the thin film away from the sides and out the opening. Do the same with the applicator top. This technique ensures easy gutta removal from a resist applicator. For efficiency, I suggest having two gutta applicators on hand so that one can be drying while another is being used.

Decorative arcylic and water-soluble resists don't harden as fast as gutta; therefore, they can be left in an applicator for longer periods of time, but the metal tip must be cleaned to prevent clogging. The best way to do this is fill an extra applicator with water and screw on the dirty top. Then shake and squeeze the applicator to flush the resist out of the tip.

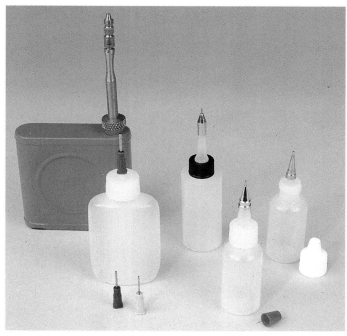

Here you see several styles of resist applicators and tips, and a solvent (gutta thinner) squirt container. The long thin nozzle on this container facilitates adding a few drops of gutta thinner to a resist applicator.

The Silkpaint Air Pen resist applicator has an electric air pump with which you activate and control the flow of the resist. It was developed for silk painters with arthritic hands and carpal tunnel syndrome, who find it difficult to squeeze the standard, plastic resist applicator.

To protect your brushes, you can purchase or make a custom brush tote, pictured here, out of a reed mat and rows of elastic. It can be rolled up for easy transport. The cotton puff in a wire clothespin and foam brushes pictured can be used to apply dye. In a classroom situation where children or adults are working in simple broad washes and salt techniques, the cotton puff and foam brushes are inexpensive tools that makes cleanup easy. For additional tools and supplies needed for wax resist techniques and screen printing, refer to chapter 7.

SILK PAINTING BRUSHES

An artist's creative needs and chosen mediums determine the types and sizes of brushes they use. Many different brushes and implements, both new and traditional, are used for silk painting. Each implement has a unique function required by a specific technique. Watercolor rounds that come to a point will help you control the flow and placement of dye as it flows from the belly of the brush. A resilient point is especially important when applying dye on to silk between resist lines. Brush hairs that separate from a point could be dragged over a resist line carrying dye into unwanted areas.

Watercolor round brushes which are made from a blend of black kazan squirrel hair and Risslon (a synthetic fiber) are a good choice for dye painting on silk. The soft squirrel hair holds a lot of dye and moves easily on the silk, while the synthetic fiber adds the body that facilitates blending and shading. The resilient and flexible point assists in controlling the application of dye between resist lines and in small, intricate areas.

For carrying a little color and blending in small areas I paint with small synthetic (Isacryl) brushes. When applying flat color and blending in larger areas bordering nooks and crannies, I recommend using a ¾-inch oval wash brush made from the resilient squirrel Risslon blend (the smaller version is often called a cat tongue). If you find you need to carry more color into your painting, switch to a larger 1″ pure squirrel oval wash and the larger squirrel-hair quill brush. This traditional quill brush used by silk painters, comes to a fine point, moves easily on the silk, and holds a lot of dye in its belly, making it easier to apply color in large areas quickly and evenly. Keep this soft floppy brush from splashing dye by holding it on the silk for a split second longer before you pick your brush up off the painting. This will stabilize the silk and the brush.

The Japanese maru-bake and the jizome-bake (page 95) are excellent tools for applying and blending ground colors that do not border on intricate resist lines. When working with a large jizome-bake, it helps to have a roller paint tray to hold the dye. When caring for your brushes, you will discover that the large natural hair brushes are a chore to clean. Many artists designate one brush for each color family, plus one each for yellow and black, so they don't require as thorough a cleaning. Other silk painters avoid this task by using inexpensive foam brushes (one for each color) for applying ground colors. Note: Unlike the jizome-bake, foam brushes will catch and drag on some textured weaves and open weaves like chiffon.

Quality brushes, if cared for properly, will last a long time. When you are in the process of painting and need to clean a brush, first rinse it in water to remove most of the dye. Then rinse in an isopropyl alcohol and water solution and again with clear water. Blot the brush and ferrule (usually metal, joining the bristles to the handle) on a towel and continue painting. Once you finish, or if you need to thoroughly clean a brush, swirl it on a wet bar of Ivory soap and gently work the lather through the hairs and rinse in tepid water. Repeat until clean. Afterward, straighten or comb out any of the center hairs that may have become tangled. Wet the brush, and shake it down so the bristles come to a point. Let the brush dry suspended so moisture drains away from the ferrule and off the point. To protect the point, never leave brushes resting in a container of water, alcohol, or dye. The brush will not only lose its shape but eventually the handle lacquer will split and peel, rotting the wood.

When storing brushes, make sure the bristles are protected from being bent out of shape. Natural-hair brushes must also be protected from silverfish, mice, and other brush-eating creatures, including household pets. To prevent rotting, never store damp brushes in airtight or plastic containers. Rather, store and transport your brushes in a brush tote that will breathe.

FABRIC STRETCHING EQUIPMENT

When you are painting on silk, the fabric must be suspended above a work surface and stretched taut. As experienced silk painters know, this is not as simple as it sounds. Once the silk becomes wet with dye it naturally loses its tautness and begins to sag and ripple. To keep the fabric from touching the work surface below it, and the dye from puddling into unwanted areas, the artist must constantly readjust the tension of the stretching method in use to maintain control of the sagging.

Shown here are two Moyer Design Fabric Stretching System models. A rolled-hem scarf is stretched on the rectangular frame in preparation for painting, while a work-in-progress is in an A–frame position ready for storage. These frames also fold and lie flat against each other. The rectangular stretcher frame will stretch silk of up to 16 by 72 inches or 32 inches square. The square stretcher frame will stretch silk of up to 45 inches square. The parts can also be assembled into two smaller frames that will accommodate fabric of up to 18 inches square. Stretcher bars of the square and rectangular frames can be combined to handle fabrics of up to 45 by 72 inches, and multiple rectangular-frame stretcher bars will take fabrics of up to 72 inches square. Each extension (not pictured) adds another yard of silk.

Other problems are "mark off" and "backstaining," which are industrial terms for uneven dyeing. Mark off occurs when the drying silk touches another surface, usually the supporting work surface or frame. Backstaining occurs when the fabric becomes stained with dye that has previously collected on equipment such as pushpins, fabric hooks, frames, or the work surface.

Silk painters work on various projects with different types of silk, all having special requirements. Silk cut from yardage, pre-hemmed scarves, and preconstructed garments all require individual attention given to the choice of frame and securing device employed. Necessity being the mother of invention, many silk painters, including myself, develop fabric-stretching devices and systems to satisfy their particular requirements.

The patented Moyer Design Fabric Stretching System can be easily and quickly adjusted to accommodate both the inconsistencies of scarf sizes and the extra stretch of crepe and other weaves.

With this system, the fabric is suspended so it never comes in contact with the frame or work surface below. While the artist works, the system automatically picks up any sagging caused by wet fabric or heavy resists. This adaptable system also enables the silk painter to stretch simple preconstructed garments such as tank tops and capes.

Legs, which slip on and off the frame, can be placed wherever needed so that even a long frame can be supported on a small tabletop. The legs can be removed at any time during the process, so you can trace, draw, stamp, stencil, and screen print a design on a flat surface. They can then be reattached to the frame, again lifting the fabric above the surface for painting.

The frame can fold with the fabric still attached, making the size more convenient for storing or transporting work in progress. This is particularly helpful for teachers and students who are demonstrating or working on projects at home and in class. The frame can also be completely disassembled for storage and traveling or it can be hung assembled (with a painting in progess) on a ladder hook in the studio.

Solutions for various fabric stretching situations and common problems

• Some fabrics like crepe de chine tend to scallop between the fabric attachment points, causing uneven tension. There are methods of stretching silk that alleviate this tension. For example, using a wide and long zigzag stitch, sew a 1½″ strip of fabric (old sheet) to each edge of your silk. Attach the silk to the stretcher via the strips. Depending upon the nature of your project, after you have stretched the silk and before you paint, either apply a resist to border the edge of the silk or on the strips that now borders the silk. This will keep the dye contained. You can also alleviate the tension by inserting stainless steel quilters' pins along the edge of the silk and then place the hooks over them. These techniques are very useful because they keep the grain of the silk straight when executing a straight border or geometric design and they help the dye to dry more evenly.

• When working on rolled hem scarves you can employ the methods described above, or place a long slim rod into the roll of the hem and attach the hooks over it, or use charted needles which are commonly used for smocking.

• When working with simple preconstructed garments that have curves, use long lai needles or similar springwire which bends to the curves and has memory. Lai needles can be purchased from some floral supply companies. Cut the eye of the needle off so it does not catch on the threads. Sand and coat them with lacquer so the metal doesn't cause rust stains.

• When painting a scarf with a rolled hem, the dye dries faster in the field than in the rolled hem. Therefore the dye starts to work its way into the drier field, causing an uneven watermark. To alleviate the uneven drying, first pinch the dye out of the hem with an absorbent paper towel, being careful not to backstain the silk with dye already collected on the towel. As the scarf continues to dry, control the flow of dye by periodically drying the hem with a hair dryer.

2 COLOR

During the silk painting process, the artist experiences color very intensely. As with many of the visual arts, this natural high is part of the allure of the silk painting medium. Another attraction is the potential for the product of this process—the colorful fabric—to be integrated into our everyday lives not only as art, but as fashion and home furnishings as well. A foundation in color theory will assist the silk painter in analyzing and using color effectively, enabling successful artistic expression whether creating for the textile industry or for personal enjoyment.

BASIC COLOR TERMS

Understanding the vocabulary of color will allow you to identify the qualities of colors; it will also help you verbalize your preferences and perceptions of color, and give you the ability to critique your own work, which is a necessary step toward any improvement. The following is a list of basic color terms. Once armed with this knowledge, you can focus on developing the more advanced technical skills.

A *primary* color is one that cannot be produced through mixing. There are only three: red, yellow, and blue. A *secondary* color is created by combining any two primary colors: yellow plus red makes orange, yellow plus blue makes green, red plus blue makes violet. A *tertiary* color is produced one of two ways: either by mixing two secondary colors, or by mixing equal parts of a primary color with a secondary color adjacent to it on the color wheel. (See below for color wheel information.)

Colors in the green, blue, and violet families are generally considered to be *cool* in temperature, while those in the red, orange, and yellow families are said to be *warm*. Adding a touch of a cool color to a warm one will make the resulting pigment less warm, and the reverse is true when adding a bit of a warm color to a cool one. For example, adding a small amount of blue to red will make the red cooler; adding a small amount of yellow to red will make the red warmer. So, even though red is generally considered a warm color, its temperature is relative—there are cool reds and warm reds.

Complements are any two colors that lie directly opposite each other on the color wheel, such as yellow and violet or red-orange and blue-green. These combinations (or harmonies) are often found in nature—for example, violets with their yellow centers, or a blue iris with an orange center, or red apples growing in (green) trees. *Analogous colors* are three to five contiguous colors on the color wheel, such as violet, blue-violet, blue, and blue-green.

A *hue* is the descriptive name of a color, such as orange, blue-violet, yellow-green, or brown. Mixing any two hues together will create a new hue; for example, red combined with blue will produce violet, and orange combined with yellow will produce a deeper yellow (or a lighter orange, depending on how you look at it). You can also mix three hues together to achieve a desired new color. Adding a fourth hue will most likely create too muddy a color, so take care when mixing.

Value is the lightness or darkness of a hue in relation to white and black, and it can be altered by adding white (or in the case of silk painting, diluent), black (pure black dye), or gray (diluent and black) in three ways:

- A hue plus white (diluent) produces a *tint* (a light value) of that hue.
- A hue plus black produces a *shade* (a dark value) of that hue.
- A tint plus black produces a *tone* (a muted, medium value) of that hue.

Intensity is how bright a hue looks. The outer ring of a color wheel shows hues at their most intense. To alter the intensity and make a color more subtle, add either a touch of its complementary color or black.

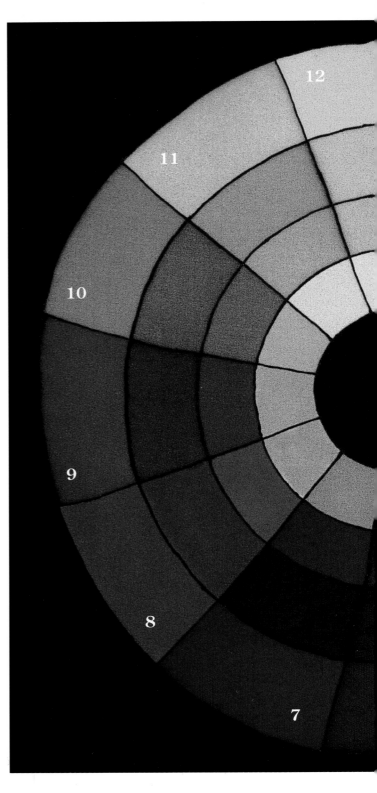

COLOR WHEEL

Making an artist's color wheel on silk is a very worthwhile project. It will serve as a reference for color harmonies, as well as for hues, tints, shades, and tones. To make one on silk, first choose a brand of dye and buy the *basic mixing colors* listed in the chart under the brand name. The basic mixing colors will provide you with hundreds of color combinations. Then follow the procedure for making the wheel which is outlined here.

Stretch a piece of silk, no smaller than 14 inches square, on a

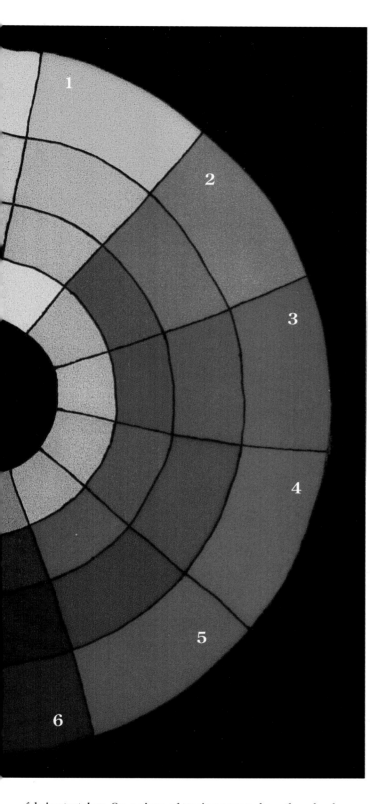

Hue Tinfix Design (Center of color wheel, Ebony Black 104)
12. yellow (Bergamont Yellow 04)
  1. yellow-orange (Bright Orange 15)
  2. warm red-orange (Coral Red 19)
  3. cool orange-red (Bengali 26)
  4. red/rhodamine (Rose Tyrian 30)
  5. red-violet/purple (Opera Purple 39)
  6. violet (Violet 41)
  7. blue-violet/reflex blue (Persian blue 49)
  8. blue/process blue (Blue Lacquer 56)
  9. green/blue-green (68 plus a little 56)
10. green/green-yellow (Permanent green 68)
11. yellow-green (mix 04 plus a little less 68)

Hue H.Dupont (Center of color wheel, Noir 700)
12. yellow (Canari 393)
  1. yellow-orange (Madrilene 406)
  2. warm red-orange (Camelia 474)
  3. cool orange-red (Cerisette 390)
  4. red/rhodamine (Grenada 502)
  5. red-violet/purple (Fuchsia 353)
  6. violet (Orchidee 386)
  7. blue-violet/reflex blue (Bleu National 362)
  8. blue/process blue (518 Ara or Blue Roy 108)
  9. green/blue-green (Emeraude 409)
10. green/green-yellow (mix 393 plus a little 518)
11. yellow-green (mix 393 plus a little less 518)

Hue Pebeo Soie (Center of color wheel, Jet Black 80)
12. yellow (Primary Yellow 01)
  1. yellow-orange (Tangerine 05 or mix 01 plus a little 07)
  2. warm red-orange (Red Poppy 07)
  3. cool orange-red (Pomegranate 15)
  4. red/rhodamine (Bougainvillaea 12)
  5. red-violet/purple (Fuchsia 09)
  6. violet (mix 12 or 09 plus a little of 28)
  7. blue-violet/reflex blue (Cobalt Blue 24)
  8. blue/process blue (Cyan 28)
  9. green/blue-green (Jade 33)
10. green/green-yellow (mix 01 plus a little 28)
11. yellow-green (mix 01 plus a little less 28)

Hue Jacquard Silk Colors *(modified fiber reactive dye)*
These highly concentrated dyes should be diluted with distilled water according to the instructions on the label.
(Center of color wheel, Black 759)
12. yellow (Yellow 703)
  1. yellow-orange (mix Yellow 703 plus a little 712)
  2. warm red-orange (Poppy Red 710)
  3. cool orange-red (Carmine Red 714)
  4. red/rhodamine (Magenta 715)
  5. red-violet/purple (Digital 117)
  6. violet (Purple 718)
  7. blue-violet/reflex blue (Royal Blue 722)
  8. blue/process blue (Cyan 725 or Turquoise 730)
  9. green/blue-green (Viridian Blue 736)
10. green/green-yellow (mix 703 plus a little 725 or 730)
11. yellow-green (mix 703 plus a little less 725 or 730)

fabric stretcher. On a piece of tracing paper, draw the wheel guidelines, dividing the circle into 12 sections and 4 concentric rings. Section 12 in the circle will correspond with 12 o'clock on a watch face. Section 1 falls immediately one space to the right at 1 o'clock, and so on. Tape this pattern to the underside of the stretched silk, and apply gutta resist following the lines of your drawing, which should show through the fabric.

Next, prepare your palette by making three sets of colors. Make up three small cups for each dye color. Use no more than ½ teaspoon of dye per cup. Label and arrange them on a tray following the order as listed above. Using the first set, apply the dye in the outer ring, beginning with section 12. Still using the first set, make the second ring of colors, which is comprised of shades of the hues, by mixing a small amount of black with each dye color. For the third ring, use the second set of colors and alter the intensity of each hue by adding a small amount of its corresponding complementary color. In the fourth ring, use the third set of colors to make tints, by mixing each hue with diluent.

WORKING WITH COLOR HARMONIES

As I travel and teach workshops around the country, I have noticed that many silk painters, including myself, limit themselves to a few favorite color combinations (or harmonies) that they use repeatedly in their artwork. These color harmonies have usually been developed through years of painting and are often very sophisticated, reflecting the artist's personal sense of style.

When I was involved in producing surface designs for the textile industry, stylists would ask me to develop patterns using specific sets of colors, often reflecting color trends not in my repertoire. Sometimes these color combinations would even offend my aesthetic sensibilities, but as I reached beyond the limitations of personal taste to work with these colors, my ability to mix, use, and appreciate color expanded. Thanks to this imposed discipline, I am now able to solve color and design problems for customers and clients who have specific requests and needs, as well as use color more effectively for my own artistic expression.

To expand your own color repertoire, I suggest you set aside the time to practice designing in various color harmonies, which are sometimes referred to as themes or schemes. Before you begin working on a design, it is best to choose the basic hues for the scheme, mix the colors, and store them in labelled jars. You can also premix the desired values and intensities, or create them as you paint. The color combinations you choose should be developed from the color theory and schemes outlined below. For these exercises, you may want to choose an abstract design so that you are better able to focus on color and composition without worrying about drawing. After this practice, the theory should become second nature to you, allowing your color expression to be intuitive, creative, and more versatile.

Monochromatic Color Scheme

For this exercise, choose a pure hue and develop a design by altering only its value and intensity. Works created with only varying tints, tones, and shades of one hue can be very dramatic. Keep in mind that active areas are created with strong contrasting values (lights and darks), while quiet areas use values that are more closely related. In silk painter Gay Lynette Morris's *Atlantic Natica* (opposite page) the darker values create a sense of depth and texture in the crevices of the shells, and these alternating lights and darks also add an interesting striped pattern.

The discipline of working with a monochromatic color scheme will help you understand how value and intensity are very basic and important aspects of composition. This also holds true when you are working in any of the other color schemes presented here.

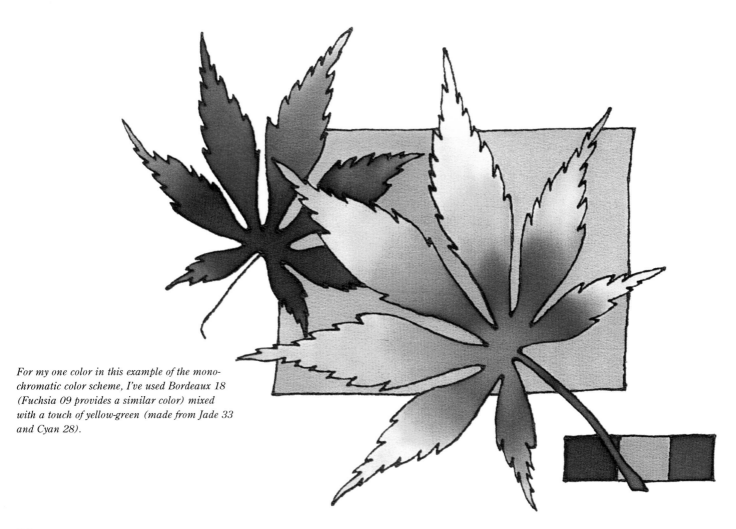

For my one color in this example of the monochromatic color scheme, I've used Bordeaux 18 (Fuchsia 09 provides a similar color) mixed with a touch of yellow-green (made from Jade 33 and Cyan 28).

ATLANTIC NATICA. © Gay Lynette Morris. *Here you see the monochromatic color scheme in use in a finished painting. The shells are all tints, tones, and shades of the same salmon-rust color.*

Complementary Color Scheme

Complementary colors are called such because, when used together, they enhance each other's value and intensity. For example, yellows are more vibrant when placed in a field of violet, and the reverse is also true. In a pair of complementary colors, one is cool and the other is warm, and when mixed together, they neutralize each other (hence the previously defined term *neutrals*). Often a successful complementary composition will include only the neutrals and very little, if any, of the pure complementary hues.

To apply this theory, choose a set of complementary colors, and premix a range of different values (tints, shades, tones) and intensities (neutrals and semi-neutrals) to work within your design. Do this exercise twice, the first time using only the neutrals and semi-neutrals (without the pure complementary hues) in your design. For your second endeavor, use the semi-neutral and neutral colors as the main colors, with the two pure complementary hues as accents. Notice how the semi-neutrals bring the pure hues to life.

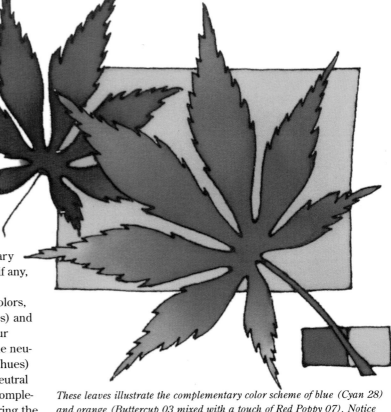

These leaves illustrate the complementary color scheme of blue (Cyan 28) and orange (Buttercup 03 mixed with a touch of Red Poppy 07). Notice how the complementary hues enhance one another.

TORCH GINGER. © Gay Lynette Morris. *The exotic red flowers against the green leaves in this beautiful silk painting demonstrate a complementary color scheme. Note, too, the use of black gutta, as an integral part of the design, to outline the flower petals and leaves.*

COLORADO FARM. © Gay Lynette Morris. *Here the artist has basically developed a complementary color scheme with neutrals to work in a landscape scene. The touch of yellow-orange against a violet-blue sky are complements, while the red roofs, blue-green hills, and yellow-green trees create a split-complementary scheme.*

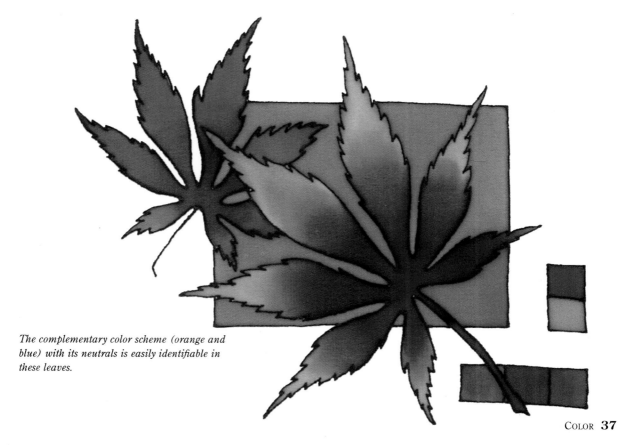

The complementary color scheme (orange and blue) with its neutrals is easily identifiable in these leaves.

Split-Complementary Color Scheme

A split-complementary scheme is achieved by introducing one complementary color to an analogous color scheme. The complement becomes the accent color in the split-complementary scheme, and can be used in very spontaneous and exciting ways to add creative spark to a design or composition. Pick either three or five analogous colors; the complementary color is the hue directly across the wheel from the middle color of your chosen sequence. For example, three analogous colors could be blue, blue-violet, and violet. The complementary color for this group would be yellow-orange.

A blue-violet, blue, and blue-green (Cobalt Blue 24, Cyan 28, and Jade 33 respectively) are used in this analogous color scheme.

The split-complementary color scheme shown here is comprised of blue-violet (Cobalt Blue 24 and a touch of Fuchsia 09), blue (Cyan 28), and blue-green (Jade 33) for the analogous colors, with an earth-tone orange (Buttercup 03 with a touch of Pomegranate 15 and Jet Black 80) for the complementary ones.

MOON RISING OVER PUEBLO.© Gay Lynette Morris. *This scene employs a split-complementary color scheme. The blue windows and doors against the orange earth tone of the buildings show a bold use of complements, while the blue-green and blue-violet hills in the background complete the scheme.*

Triad Color Scheme

Color triads are composed of three colors that are equidistant from each other on the color wheel. There are only four basic combinations: the primary colors —red, yellow, and blue; the secondary colors—orange, violet, and green; and two sets of tertiary colors—yellow-orange, red-violet, and blue-green, and red-orange, blue-violet, and yellow-green. Triads used in varying tints, tones, shades, and intensities make dynamic and interesting combinations. For drama and strength in a design, one color of the triad should dominate, with the other two used in unequal proportions.

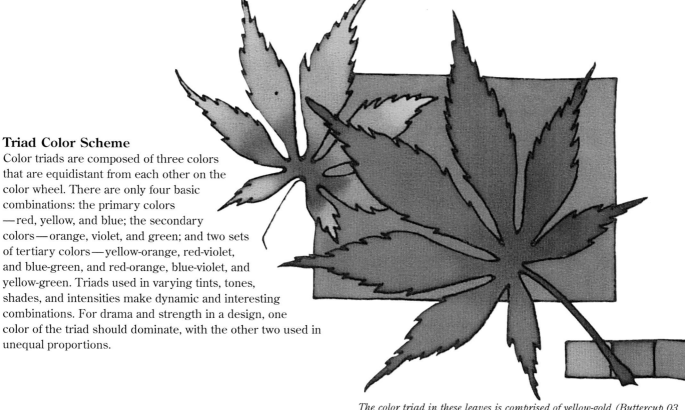

The color triad in these leaves is comprised of yellow-gold (Buttercup 03 and a touch of Jet Black 80), blue-green (Jade 33 with a bit of Primary Yellow 01), and red-violet (Fuchsia 09).

JERICHO. © Gay Lynette Morris. *The predominant use of the red, yellow, and blue color triad, along with the corresponding neutrals, brings this color composition together.*

Dominant Hue Color Scheme

Using a dominant hue is another way to unify a painting. Natural light seems to harmonize our surroundings by imbuing them with a small amount of the same color. This dominant hue brings all the colors into harmony and creates a mood. For example, a landscape bathed in the light of a sunset will take on a reddish cast; on a rainy day the landscape will take on a blue-violet cast.

In silk painting, many colors are often mixed by overpainting (painting one color over another on the silk) and the use of a dominant hue will integrate the design, slightly neutralizing and reducing the intensity of any unmixed hues in the composition. Your colors will be richer, earthier, and more coordinated once you become more familiar with the dominant hue theory and apply it to your silk painting.

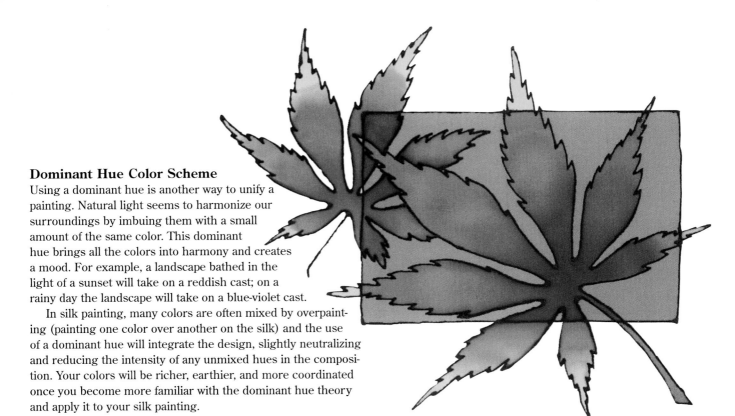

Here a tone of sky blue (Cyan 28 and Cobalt Blue 24 diluted and mixed with a touch of Jet Black 80) is the dominant hue placed over blends of Bougainvillea 12, Buttercup 03, sky blue (undiluted and without black), and Primary Yellow 01. It ties all the colors together and makes them a bit more subtle.

MISTY MORNING. © Len Brondum. *The dominant blue-violet hue creates a unifying atmosphere of early morning mist in the air and dampness on the forest floor.*

40 COLOR

RUSSIA, SCUZDAL. © Natashe Foucault. *The dominant reddish hues of this roofscape create a sunset atmosphere over this chilly, Russian winter scene.*

Random Color Scheme

This kind of scheme is the most difficult to execute and control because there are no rules. It is also difficult to emulate. On occasion, a stylist would point out a random color scheme in a fashion magazine and ask me to use those colors in my collection of designs. I found it quite a creative challenge to develop compositions this way. On analyzing works in which color was used in a seemingly random way, I noticed that many such compositions were actually based on either a dominant complementary or a split-complementary scheme; some compositions even incorporated multiple color schemes. Inevitably, almost any color will work with another, given the right proportions, placement, and variety of shapes in a composition.

When working with a random color scheme, silk painters often begin a piece by painting motifs and images on a white ground. Since the colors are positioned randomly against this ground, the trick is choosing and mixing a background color that will set off all the hues while maintaining an overall balance. Grays, cool beiges, other neutrals, or black are often good solutions because they provide a quiet supporting ground and subtly set off all the random colors without matching or detracting from any of them. They can also be used in a border to frame and control a random scheme.

For an experienced designer, decisions on color and placement are made through a combination of personal taste and aesthetic intuition. Therefore, the most creative way to develop a design for a random color palette is to practice and work intuitively with your chosen premixed colors. When I find myself challenged by a color scheme (What hue should I use in the background? How should I balance the elements of this composition?), I refer to my collection of color swatches and to my experience in color theory and design for visual support. Although it is risky, working with this type of scheme satisfies a creative need and gives me the opportunity to strengthen my artistic judgments as well as learn from my design successes and failures.

Once you have expanded your knowledge of color by applying the various harmonies to several designs, you will be ready to take greater risks and use your creative intuition in developing or emulating random color schemes.

NOAH'S ARK. © Gay Lynette Morris. *The daughter of a missionary, Gay has drawn from the familiar teachings of her childhood to recreate this biblical scene with tropical patterns and motifs. This is the first in a series of Noah's Ark scenes that has been reproduced as limited edition posters. Here, the use of repeated shapes and a random color scheme adds variety and keeps the eye moving throughout the painting. The neutral, black and white border acts as a frame for the scene; it contrasts with the random color scheme, but the abstract pattern keeps it tied into the design.*

BUTTERFLY FISH.© Gay Lynette Morris. *This piece employs a random color scheme, but as you study it you can also see Gay's intentional and strong use of complementary (red against green) and split-complementary (yellow against blue-violet, violet, and red-violet) schemes within the total composition. Like most accomplished artists, she uses color both to articulate form and to provide compositional balance.*

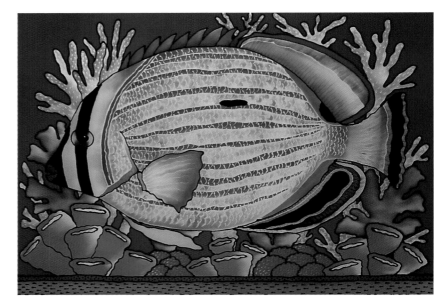

LORIKEETS (detail). © Linda France Hartge and David Hartge. *Linda's beautiful color schemes are often seemingly random in nature, but on closer examination her strong use of complementary and split-complementary colors within the overall composition becomes apparent. Like* Butterfly Fish *(opposite page), this detail juxtaposes red against green and yellow-orange against blue-violet.*

3 BUILDING A FOUNDATION

Silk painting has the ability to satisfy our intrinsic need to develop and express ourselves as artists. This is one of its greatest beauties. People with little, if any, previous art experience are drawn to the medium and enthusiastically learn basic techniques. Then, stimulated by the seemingly endless possibilities and challenges of working with silk, they delve into more creative projects.

Technical skills are essential to the growth of an artist and to success in the undertaking of more advanced endeavors. Silk painters must make a commitment to acquire and improve their design and composition abilities. And, since the balance of skills and challenge is essential to the growth of an artist, I am always inspired when my students strive to interpret new subject matter or express new moods, rather than simply ask, "What else can I do with salt and alcohol techniques?" At this point, I can sense that they are beginning to grasp the diversity and potential of the medium and are ready to confront new goals.

WHITE RHODODENDRON. © Evelyn Jenkins Drew

DEVELOPING DESIGN IDEAS

I often recommend that the novice artist enroll in color and design, drawing, or painting courses. These basic art classes teach the meaning of line, form, space, texture, and color — the fundamental elements of design. While studying these concepts in relation to composition, the principles of art — balance, pattern and repetition, rhythm, movement, and contrast — will also be discovered. It is also in these classes that individual design ideas and preferences begin to surface.

This recommendation may seem somewhat intimidating. While silk painting is definitely an art, people who become interested in it don't necessarily think of themselves as artists or as having the ability to become artists. But experience as both a teacher and student has taught me that knowledge and mastery are learned, not inherited. Individual aptitudes for art may determine the ease or difficulty with which you develop artistic capabilities, but ultimately, motivation and discipline are the keys to artistic growth. Time spent honing basic design skills is well invested, because ability and creativity often improve with age.

Research is one of the best ways to learn and gather ideas. Fashion, interior design, and fine art magazines are a good source of many motifs and color schemes. These ideas can then be combined in a fabric design, garment, or painting in new and creative ways. As artists develop, so do their research processes. For example, you might find yourself frequenting museums or clothing boutiques; craft fairs are also educational because, like art classes, they afford the opportunity to see what other artists are doing. Eventually, you will tailor your methods of research to suit your individual needs and style. Once you have this foundation, your medium will become a less-intimidating source of inspiration.

EXPLORING DESIGN THROUGH DRAWING

When people ask me where I get my own inspiration, my first response is, "drawing." Drawing is a crucial form of artistic research and development. As you learn to draw, you learn to see and understand your environment from a different and more visual, aesthetic perspective. And, you learn how to communicate visually. Many artists speak of this process as becoming "visually literate." Just as hearing music through a musician's ear, and with a musician's knowledge, can only heighten the listening experience, the ability to see with an artist's eye can only enhance one's life and art.

As a discipline, drawing will inspire you and teach you many interesting ways to interpret subject matter. It will help you discover or better observe the textures and spatial relationships occurring in the environment. The natural patterns, rhythms, and contrasts found all around us are the very elements we need to inspire our compositions. But you are only as good as your drawing ability, because, as with any language, you can express yourself only up to your level of development, whatever it may be. Whether composing an abstract or a representational image, don't let your ideas be held at the mercy of your drawing skills; it is to your advantage to improve this craft so that you can communicate in any way and at any level you choose.

Artist Linda France Hartge's exquisitely designed and drawn silk paintings clearly illustrate the influence of nature on the artist and the importance of drawing. While doing research, she and her partner David Hartge of Kaleidosilk became interested in a species of carp known as koi. These fish are bred for form and color by the Japanese to grace their water gardens. Linda translated the textures and patterns she discovered while observing the koi in their lily ponds into her designs; and as she researched and painted them, her interest in the fish became more intense. Both Linda and David were so fascinated by their subject matter that they became active members of a club devoted to studying and breeding award winning, beautifully marked and proportioned koi. Linda pays such close attention to detail in her drawings that koi enthusiasts have recognized the champion koi, called Tancho Sanshoku, in her painting *Tancho* (on the page opposite).

CLOWN TRIGGER. © Linda France Hartge and David Hartge. *Drawing is a form of observation and of gathering information. Linda observed and was truly inspired by the fish's combinations of bold motifs and colors, which are not merely decorative but function as natural protective camouflage from predators. Her drawing and design skills enabled her to convey the patterns and rhythms found in nature.*

TANCHO. © Linda France Hartge and David Hartge. *Linda used the champion koi, Tancho Sanshoko, as a reference when composing this painting. Once she understood the fish's basic form, she eliminated some of its natural elements and enhanced others, effectively stylizing her image. For example, the ripples that surround Tancho have been stylized. Due to her familiarity with the subject through observation and drawing, Linda was still able to preserve the essence of the fish despite any artistic liberty she may have taken. For this reason, koi enthusiasts can identify Tancho and consider the painting an unofficial portrait.*

KOI GARDEN (screen). © Linda France Hartge and David Hartge. *These lines are so seductively drawn, the colors so rich, and the perspective so inviting that the viewer can't help but think he is actually standing on a footbridge overlooking this pond. To create a painting with such feeling involves a combination of drawing, composition, and silk painting skills. Linda first explored her subject (the Japanese garden pond) by sketching it. To counteract the vertical thrust of the screen frames, she devised a composition that placed images horizontally across the separate sections, ultimately creating three horizontal movements to balance the three vertical screen panels. The slightly diagonal cat-o'-nine-tails near the edges of the painting stop the horizontal flow and keep the eye within the painting. The vertical and diagonal positions of the koi also interrupt the lateral motion. The lily pads float on the pond surface and create a sense of space and depth. They also move toward the viewer, inviting him into the scene.*

BLUE HERONS RISING. © Len Brondum. *The repeated image of the cat-o'-nine-tails creates vertical lines to contrast the circular grid that flows throughout this painting. Len uses the structure of this grid, which emulates ripples in a pond, to break down her shapes, colors, and composition, creating an abstraction of the forms found in nature.*

TULIPS. © Ute Patel-Missfeldt. *In this unusual image, Ute combines both a realistic and a stylized representation of the tulip. The flowers above ground are accurately drawn, twisting and reaching for the sunlight much as they would in nature. It is below the surface that the more two-dimensional, stylized design occurs in the oval-shaped bulbs with their radiating halos of color and stiff, projecting roots. This stylization effectively highlights the difference between what is above and what is below the earth's surface. From the book* Jugendstils, *published by Eulen Verlag.*

EXPLORING ABSTRACTION

Rather than focusing on realistic depictions of objects, silk painters like Suzanne Punch explore the elements of design and principles of art purely for their own sakes. This type of expression, called abstract art, requires experience (in both figurative and abstract representation) and a willingness to aggressively explore the potential of the medium.

Suzanne pays special attention to the negative space—the background or areas between the motifs—in her floral paintings and garments. In these compositions, this negative space is always vibrant, well designed, and in balanced proportion to the positive areas (the subject matter or motif). As a result, the entire piece is more harmonious when finished. In her abstract paintings, she focuses on the spatial concerns of merging texture, color, and shape to create the illusion of deep space. This quality of joining space from different planes in a two-dimensional medium is called *plasticity*. Without this there is no sense of depth, and the forms remain forever floating on the picture (or surface) plane. To create a feeling of three dimensionality, Suzanne uses the inherent whiteness of the silk as the lightest value and creates her space relationships with multiple layers of dye and resist.

Color and light are integral tools in creating the illusion of depth and can be used in many ways. In some cases, lighter hues bring images or spaces closer to the foreground, or picture plane, of a painting. This occurs with the bright fish in artist Jacqueline Noss-Ferrero's *The Comedians* (see page 53), which swim right up to the viewer and are set off by the deeper, receding tones of the water; the dark colors of the water also lead the eye back further into the scene. The opposite is true in artist Natashe Foucault's *Winter in Weaverville* (see page 53). In this windowsill still life, reminiscent of photorealism in its representational style, the darker, interior areas of the foreground are closer to the viewer, while the lighter snowscape pulls the eye out into the distance.

For Linda and Suzanne, and all these artists, inspiration comes from pursuing a deeper understanding of the creative process and the relationship between their environment and their medium. The devoted interest of a koi enthusiast for a certain fish, or the appreciation an avid gardener has for a particular flower, is essentially the same passion for color and form. Since they have developed their technical skills as silk painters, these artists are able to express their involvement with their subject matter visually through their art.

FAST WATERS AT GIVERNY. © Suzanne Punch. *Here, resist is used to suggest the rapid movement and undercurrents of water. After creating this initial feeling of motion, the challenge for Suzanne is to suspend the areas of warm color in the midst of all that fluid coolness. Although warm colors usually convey energy and vibration, here they create islands of calm (resembling reflective patches of sunlight) that contrast the direction of the diagonal resist strokes.*

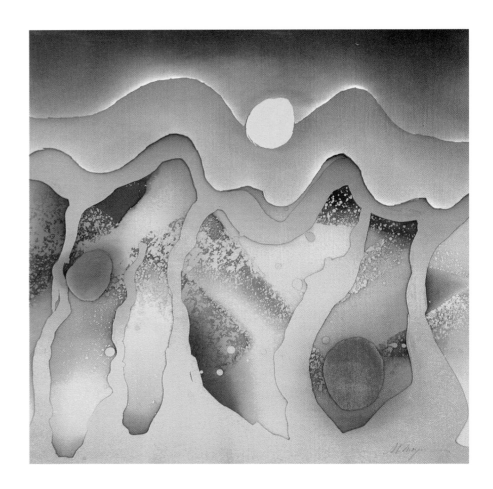

Na Pali Coast. © Susan Louise Moyer. *When we view art, we subconsciously bring our previous visual history into that present moment. These past experiences provide a context within which we automatically assume and expect certain things to be true. In this painting, the strong horizontal divisions with blue above, which we will always see as sky, lead us to read the abstract elements below as the rugged and eroded coast, with all of its nooks and crannies, bathed in the sun of a tropical paradise. If the painting were to be turned upside down, the blue horizontal would be seen as the ocean reflecting the light of the moon or sun. Any surrounding elements, no matter how abstract, will also be incorporated into that interpretation.*

Bridge II. © Suzanne Punch. *Using a technique much like the action painting pioneered by Jackson Pollock in the 1960s, Suzanne literally flings dye and resist at the silk with no preconceived notions about composition. In doing so, she challenges herself to explore her own creative potential in relation to the behavior of the medium. She also relies on the intuitive expression of her artistic skills for color and formal solutions. In this case, the light lines of white resist provide highlights, and the central dark, arching lines become a "bridge" that serves as both a visual and psychological escape from the menacing areas of the foreground. This bridge also creates depth as it guides the eye back and forth from the larger, warm-hued shapes in the front to the receding, cool-colored shapes in the distance.*

THE COMEDIANS. © Jacqueline Noss-Ferrero. *This whimsical painting combines representational drawing with abstraction. The fish, although stylized and slightly comical, are expressive and fairly realistic. In the background, on the other hand, Jacqueline explores abstract impressions of the forms, textures, space, and light found in the ocean environment. To do this she combines salt, alcohol, and wet-on-wet techniques, which all help to emulate the feel of deep ocean water. The salt technique involves placing salt crystals on freshly painted silk. The salt pulls the wet dye in various directions, creating interesting swirls and shapes. The alcohol technique also produces unusual patterns when droplets of alcohol diluent are carefully splattered on a painted ground. In the wet-on-wet technique the silk is first dampened with alcohol diluent and then decorated with dye. In this way, the shapes of color spread slowly and dry with a softer edge.*

WINTER IN WEAVERVILLE. © Natashe Foucault. *Natashe creates a mood and multiple planes by contrasting realistic and abstract elements. The clear, cozy interior is distinctly separate from the icy, obscure landscape behind it. The warm hues and expertly drawn objects invite the viewer into a homey, familiar environment and focus attention on this foreground space, which is very close to the picture plane. By comparison, the cool colors of the hazy background pull this space even further into the distance.*

4 SURFACE DESIGN

Silk painters often use their original fabric designs to create fashions and home furnishings. Knowing and using a specific "layout," called a surface design, that is conducive to your application will help you achieve more finished, professional-looking results. Surface designs provide guidelines that help you solve specific visual and placement problems when creating a layout. Artists who understand surface design layouts create patterns that are both unique and consistent in quality, and in the process, they also cut down on fabric waste.

It is important for the silk painter to understand the design principles behind these layouts. Form should follow function, not compete with it. Just as the shape of a garment is constructed to flow with and flatter a person's figure, so should the surface design. For instance, a vertical stripe on a skirt may be more flattering than a horizontal one, which widens the figure. The same is true for home furnishings; the surface pattern should work with the object's intended use. For example, fabrics with vertical stripes are more appropriate for draperies because the direction of the motif gives an increased sense of height to the room and windows.

BLACK, WHITE, AND COLOR (detail). © Joanell Connolly. Photo by the artist

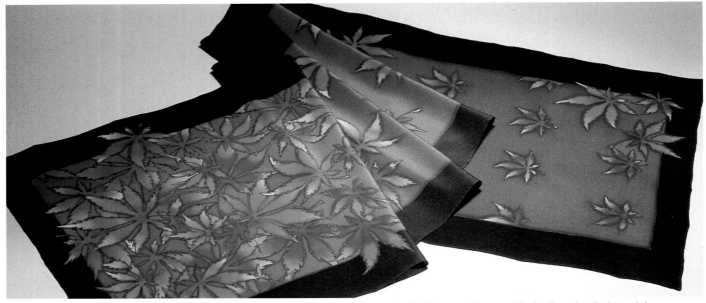

FALLING LEAVES. © Susan L. Moyer. *This scarf employs the various motif placements described here, as illustrated in the three details shown below.*

THE THREE BASIC LAYOUTS

There are three basic ways to orient the elements, or motif, in a surface design. This placement is referred to as the layout. Elements can all be placed in the same direction, in other words with their tops and bottoms pointing the same way; or, they can be placed in different directions, meaning their tops and bottoms face different ways. In the following descriptions and the three illustrations (shown below), I use a leaf motif to indicate direction or orientation (and also lack thereof). These layouts apply to most other motifs as well. The three basic layouts are:

- *allover nondirectional* (no top or bottom): leaves are scattered all over with stems facing in all directions; the layout will work any way.

- *allover one-directional* (top and bottom): leaves are scattered all over with stems facing either up or down; the layout will work only one way.

- *two-directional* (top and bottom reversible): leaves are scattered with some stems facing up and others facing down; the layout will work two ways.

Besides being oriented in a certain direction, the motifs in a design are often carefully spaced, and this also contributes to the overall surface design layout. The basic arrangements are as follows:

- *tossed:* there is some ground, or space, between the individual elements — in this case, the leaves.

Here, the three top rows of leaves are placed in a one-directional set motif, which then changes to a two-directional set motif in the next two rows.

In the middle of this section of the scarf a one-directional tossed motif is used.

Moving toward the end of the scarf, the design incorporates a nondirectional tossed motif, which gradually becomes a nondirectional packed motif at the very bottom with only a little background visible.

TOUCAN AND PARROT. © Susan L. Moyer. *This silk painting makes use of nondirectional and two-directional layouts. The crescents are nondirectional and the leaves and zigzag stripes are two-directional.*

- *packed:* little, if any, ground appears between the elements of the motif.
- *set:* the motif is set in rows either vertically or horizontally, or it is arranged symmetrically.

More than one type of layout can be incorporated in a design. For example, an allover nondirectional leaf motif can be tossed over a ground pattern such as a texture or stripe. In my painting

Toucan and Parrot (above), three layouts are incorporated into one surface design: the crescent shapes are placed in a tossed and nondirectional manner, the leaves are tossed in a two-directional layout, and the zigzag stripes are also two-directional. For more examples, explore the latest fashions and fabrics, and try to identify the layouts employed by a range of surface designers. As you work with the following basic design exercises, you will begin to see that infinite variations are possible.

WORKING WITH DESIGN

These exercises teach the principles behind surface design layouts and the guidelines for executing them. They utilize basic geometric shapes in a tossed layout. It may take time and practice to get to the point at which these principles become intuitive, so be patient. Perseverance will give you a foundation for an endless amount of design ideas and will enable you to creatively break the rules to produce more successful, professional-looking wearable art and home-furnishing fabrics.

Materials

18- by 24-inch tracing paper (pad or roll)

pencils

kneaded eraser

T square

right angle

scissors

clear tape

In addition, you might find these optional design aids helpful:

Bodice template. Shaped like the front of a size 8 strapless bodysuit, the template is placed over a surface design to check if the size, placement, and direction of the motif elements compliment the shape of the body.

Proportion wheel. Used by graphic designers, the proportion wheel helps you calculate the amount by which you need to reduce or enlarge a particular motif when adapting its size to the proportions of the garment or other project you're incorporating it into. It is most helpful when you are enlarging or reducing a design on a copy machine and need the actual percentage. For example, if you have a motif that is 2½ inches wide and you want to enlarge it to 4¾ inches, the proportion wheel will determine that 4¾ is 190 percent of 2½; therefore, you would enlarge a 2½ inch motif 190 percent (on the copier) to make it 4¾ inches. Likewise, the wheel would tell you that to adapt a motif that appears on a 36-inch-square scarf to the proportions of a 45-inch-square scarf, you would enlarge the motif by 125 percent.

The Exercises

Draw all the basic design shapes — circles, squares, triangles, and crescents — on a piece of tracing paper and then cut them out. You will probably need at least 20 of each shape. For each layout type, experiment with the placement of the various shapes, using another sheet of paper as your practice background surface. Move the shapes around, perhaps even overlapping them. To give yourself ample space, each practice surface should be no smaller than 18 by 22 inches. Once you are satisfied with your layouts, affix the motifs to the paper with tape. Remember to use the bodice template to check the movement of each layout.

Try all of the following:

- allover nondirectional circles in a tossed layout
- allover nondirectional squares in a tossed layout
- allover nondirectional triangles in a tossed layout
- allover nondirectional crescents or curved lines in a tossed layout
- allover nondirectional combined shapes in a tossed layout
- allover nondirectional motif with a directional motif. One example of this layout might incorporate stripes (directional motif) with tossed (nondirectional) circles.

A bodice template cut from black paper is placed over sketches of two nondirectional surface designs to see if the layout will flatter a woman's silhouette.

Snapshots were used as a drawing reference for a floral motif, and the proportion wheel was then used to determine the percentage of reduction or enlargement of the elements to be incorporated into the design and layout.

AUTUMN GEOMETRY. © Merridee Joan Smith. *Using stamps she made out of polymer clay, Merridee laid out a non-directional wax resist design consisting of geometric shapes and ginkgo leaves over a lightly blended ground. Notice how she placed her motifs. They float up and over the right shoulder, down and across the lower left back and around to the lower left front, leaving a lot of negative space on the left side of the jacket. To play pattern against pattern she then waxed and painted a two-directional grid over the entire piece. This process created a very unique surface design with color movement and contrasts of pattern that not only add interest to the jacket but the surface design layout on the garment also compliments the body when worn.*

MAUNA LOA. © Susan Louise Moyer. Model: Dale Moyer. *This Aloha shirt was inspired by the active volcano on the big island of Hawaii. The fabric was designed and executed so the shirt pattern could be spot placed on the boarder of the yardage. This surface design incorporates a combination of directional stripes, tossed spots and contrasting bands of color and texture along the borders.*

Guidelines for placement of motifs in a surface design layout for garments

• Keep the eye moving throughout the design. Awkward placement of motifs distracts the eye. On an article of clothing, this might be the unflattering effect created when a motif falls on each breast or on the backside. To avoid these occurrences, make sure the size, positioning, and spacing of the motifs do not create a strong horizontal or vertical. This happens when three or more motifs end up in a horizontal or vertical line or when the size of the motif and the space between the motifs are not considered.

• Work with an odd number of elements (three, five, seven).

• Avoid large spiky motifs, like stiff palm leaves or geometric shapes, which will visually cut the body silhouette and stop eye movement.

• One way to create a feeling of motion is to add curves to the motifs. A simple example would be curving the stems of leaves and flowers in a tossed layout.

• Keep the negative space (background shape between the motifs) balanced and interesting by varying the size and placement of the individual motifs.

• Use the bodice template (page 58) to check all of the above aspects of the design and layout.

• In design, there are always exceptions to the guidelines. Understanding the reason behind the "rule" will help you create a successful exception. Some creative exceptions become trends.

Untitled. © 2003 Suzanne Perilman. Photo by Pat Pollard. *Trained as a graphic designer as well as a fiber artist, Suzanne collects antique Japanese hand-cut paper stencil patterns and motifs from kimono factories and makes the stencils into photo silkscreens. She then transforms her collection into new and current fashions. This kimono jacket is made out of silk organza which brings the traditional kimono into the early twenty-first century. Suzanne's creative process involves several steps. She paints, screens, and discharges the fabric, spot places her patterns, cuts the fabric, and has the garment constructed. Working/thinking three-dimensionally, she continues her creative process by discharging and adding motifs to the already constructed garment. For example the red fan, which is placed off center toward the right shoulder, was added to balance the red collar and brings your eye upward.*

Untitled. © 2002 Suzanne Perilman. Photo by Pat Pollard. *In this piece, Suzanne has taken the old and made it new again by coordinating one of her own wax resist designs with accents of antique Japanese stencil patterns and motifs. In Suzanne's line of wearable art her well-placed and well-drawn signature, as you see here on the obi, is a wonderful accent to her designs. But be aware that a signature that is not well placed or well drawn may suggest that the garment was less then professionally designed. Her work reflects a discerning choice of color, classic styling, and graphic placement of the various patterns and motifs.*

DRAGON DANCE © 2003 Elaine Nobuko Gima. Photo by Tony Novak-Clifford. Model: Jamie Roth. *Brushed resist and procion dyes on 3 ply crepe de chine silk. Elaine, who was born in the Hawaiian Islands, lives and paints in her studio on Maui. Elaine enjoys "depicting nature's essence: the life force." Her beautiful tunic dress is a fabulous example of an engineered design. Notice the placement of the surf as it comes over the shoulder around the collar, subtly echoing the neckline. The wave continues as it moves across the chest, then angling almost straight down and around the hem line. The design is dramatic and the engineering has been kept simple.*

Elaine, with the experience and skill of a master, let her water-soluble linear resist break down under the application of dye. By allowing the color to flow in and out of the weakened resist lines, she depicted the "life force" of the powerful and beautiful crashing waves. Her execution captures the motion of the surf and enhances the form of the body.

FARBRAUSCH. © Ute Patel-Missfeldt. *Ute develops both her garments and surface design in one creative process. The bodice, collar, sleeves, and belt were constructed out of her original pattern and engineered surface design. The artist drew the surface design on the pattern pieces prior to painting to ensure that the images would fall in the desired places once the garment was constructed. From the book* Seidenmonde mit Phantasie, *published by Eulen Verlag.*

PLANNING SURFACE DESIGNS FOR FASHION

There are two main ways to design fabric that is intended for wearable art, with several variations dictated by process and creativity. The first is to spot place the garment pattern pieces on a chosen area of your original painted silk. Using the design and layout information on pages 56-59 to guide you in executing a surface design will insure success when spot placing. The second method is to engineer a design where the elements are placed to move with and complement the lines of a specific garment and body silhouette. The fabric is then painted accordingly.

When developing an engineered design, it important to consider how the motif will fall on the body as well as where it falls on the pattern, for ease of execution. A design that incorporates a motif that flows from the bodice of a dress onto a sleeve, or from the front of a jacket onto the back, may have a motif that falls on a seam. If so, it is best to keep that part of the design that bridges a seam simple and less intricate.

To execute an engineered design, first determine the size and configuration of the fabric stretchers you will need to layout and paint all the pattern pieces at the same time, plus some extra. Also, preshrink the unpainted silk so that the pattern size will not shrink during the steaming process. Then stretch your silk onto your fabric stretchers and set aside (see chapter 1).

Dress. © Marcuse. Photo by Lindy Powers. *The bodice of this dress is constructed from fabric with a nondirectional, set design that has been machine smocked. The grid effect floating over the blue skirt is created both by vertical stripes constructed out of handpainted fabric and horizontal strips constructed from a coordinating fabric. The bright, vibrating colors enhance the effect of this already dramatic concept.*

Quilted Peacock Jacket. © Linda France Hartge and David Hartge. *Another example of an engineered design, this jacket also incorporates machine embroidery and quilting. The stitching adds texture and dimension to the design. Note that Linda avoids absolute symmetry by placing the eyes of the feathers at different heights on each side of the jacket.*

Draw the intended design and all of its elements on a fabric pattern, preferably made with fabric that has a similar drape to the weave and weight of silk you have chosen to paint. Baste the seams together and place the sample garment on the intended body form. Check the fit of the pattern and the placement of the design, make the necessary adjustments, and remove the stitches. Transfer the design and any fit adjustments to a paper pattern.

Depending on your design and techniques, you may need to paint a ground first. Otherwise, proceed by placing the individual pattern pieces under your silk. Be sure the guide lines (found on the original pattern) are lined up correctly with the grain of the silk. Trace the pattern outline and design onto the silk using a chalk fabric pencil. After removing the pattern pieces, start executing your design onto the silk with your chosen resist.

For consistency of color and execution, finish all of the sections that are in the same coloration and technique before going onto the next application. It is also wise to paint some extra fabric for creative options, for example, if you decide you need to add trim. Once you have finished painting and have steam set the dye, complete the garment by following the sewing instructions supplied with the commercial pattern. If you don't sew, you can employ a professional seamstress to adjust the pattern fit before painting and then construct the painted garment for you.

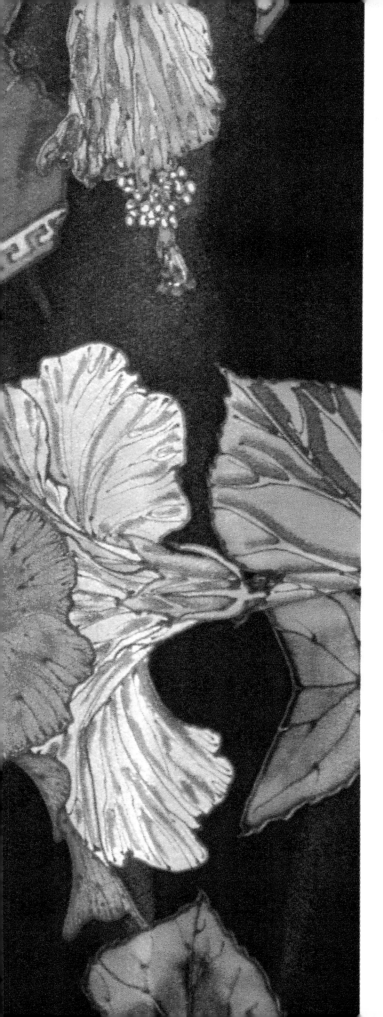

5 FASHION AND FASHION ACCESSORY PROJECTS

When designing functional objects such as scarves, pillows, and ties, always remember the architect Louis Sullivan's guiding principle: form ever follows function. This dictum was adopted by the Bauhaus, a school of architecture and design founded in Germany in the early 1920s, whose main artistic goal was to attain a synthesis of technology, craftsmanship, and design aesthetics. Silk painters, too, must know how to plan specific projects and handle the silk so they can design and construct fashions and fashion accessories that are practical as well as beautiful. The information in this chapter is intended to provide the foundation for creating successful work.

HIBISCUS AND STAR CHART SCARF (detail). © Linda France Hartge and David Hartge

Fire and Ice. © Susan L. Moyer. *Wax resist was placed over both thickened and unthickened dyes to create the design on this scarf. The border, which is an integral part of the composition, was created with wax resist brushstrokes.*

SCARVES

A scarf is the perfect canvas for the silk painter and a versatile accessory for its owner. Fashions continue to evolve with the times, but scarves have long been and probably always will be luxurious yet practical accessories. Scarves make wonderful gifts. They can be romantic, chic, functional, or festive. They frame the face and create or enhance a fashion mood. Any silk weave is appropriate for a scarf and each has its own unique feel: chiffon is light and airy, charmeuse is luxurious and sensuous, crepe has a beautiful drape and a subtle sheen.

Designing a Scarf

When planning a scarf design layout, many beginning silk painters arrange the main image or motif details in the center field of the scarf and frame the composition with a wide but simple straight border. As a result, when the scarf is draped around the neck or over a shoulder, the painting becomes lost in the folds, leaving only the simple border exposed. Therefore, if you are creating a scarf that is to be used as a fashion accessory rather than a painting, it may be wiser to plan a more interesting border with a simple central field. In this way, your design will

OCEAN KELP. © 2003 Susan Louise Moyer.
The kelp motif was drawn in clear gutta resist and painted over an ombre ground. Color was also removed to create highlights. The line building technique creates the underwater effect on the ends of the scarf.

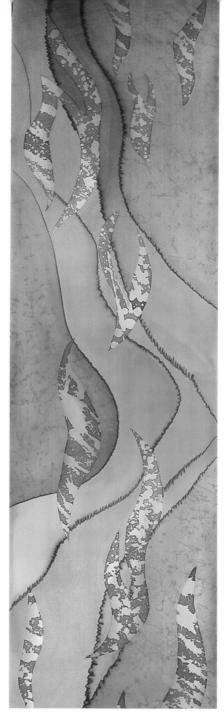

PASSAGES. © 2003 Susan Louise Moyer.
Starting with the line-building technique on an ombre ground, wax was applied to protect the negative space and color was removed from the shapes with alcohol diluent. The shapes were then painted and waxed and painted again, creating a playfull effect of directional and nondirectional patterns on a directional ground.

PATCHES II. © 2002 Susan Louise Moyer.
Starting with the line-building technique on an ombre ground, patches of spontaneous directional and nondirectional patterns were applied using wax and dye.

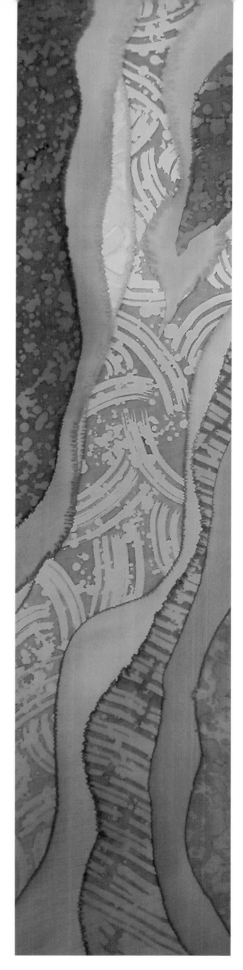

FRINGED CAT. © Judith Bateman and Suzanne Bateman-Smith. *The border on this scarf is effectively integrated with the overall design.*

MORNING GLORY AND BAMBOO. © Linda France Hartge and David Hartge. *The bold colors in this scarf make it a striking fashion accessory.*

not be lost in fabric folds. The main field can still be full of subtle textures, colors, and patterns that will echo the border design and compliment and frame the face, but the more visible border should be the most intricate area. Be creative. When planning a border, keep in mind the shape of your scarf. What design elements should fall on the corners of a square scarf and on the ends of an oblong or rectangular scarf? Rather than repeating the same images and colors on each corner, paint these areas to complement each other. As silk painter Linda France Hartge points out, "Scarves often have distinctive images in each corner, often with a narrative relationship between them."

Rolled Scarf Hems

The hemmed edges of scarves are traditionally hand-rolled; the end of the fabric is rolled in once or twice and then lightly slip-stitched in place by hand. A slip stitch is one in which the thread picks up only a few fibers of the fabric to hold the hem in place; in this way, the stitches are hardly visible on the right side of the garment. The rolled edge of a scarf should have an even roundness and should not be ironed flat. Unfortunately, steam-setting the dyes and ironing out wax resist, techniques that are often part of the silk-painting process, will flatten this hem. Therefore, the only way to truly maintain the round shape is to hem the scarf only after all silk-painting and dye-setting processes are complete.

However, to conserve time, I work on scarf blanks, which are prehemmed silk scarves available in some fabric and sewing supply stores and catalogues. Even though the hems may be flattened while steaming and ironing, they are often restored to a rounder shape in the final steps of the finishing process (the washing and dry cleaning). Whenever dry cleaning, I request that the rolled hem not be pressed.

SCARF WITH BUCK AND PHEASANTS. © Antoinette von Grone. *The plain border on this scarf frames and sets off the central composition.*

APPLE VEST JACKET. © Linda France Hartge and David Hartge. *The layout of this garment was carefully engineered so that the apple motif would fall in a predetermined area, in this case the center of the back, making it a main design element.*

PILLOWS

Pillows, like scarves, can be earthy or elegant, whimsical or classical, the main event or a simple accent. With the proper choice of fabric and careful thought given to design, a painted-silk pillow can add a perfect decorative touch to almost any room.

Choosing the fabric is the first step. Again, keep in mind that form follows function. Will the pillow actually be used, or will it be purely decorative? Hence, which fabric weight is more appropriate? It has been my experience that pillow covers made from medium- to heavyweight silks (12mm and up) have more body, are more durable, and are easier to construct. The result is a more professional-looking pillow. Lighter silks (5mm to 10mm) are not as opaque as heavier-weight silks and should be backed with a white fabric or white fusible.

Pillows can be almost any size or shape imaginable, but the most common is the knife-edge pillow. This is a pillow that can be made into almost any shape on which the front and back panel edges are joined with a simple seam. For the projects and suggestions in this section, I have worked with a square knife-edge pillow style.

Guidelines for Basic Pillow Design

Since the sides of most pillows slope down, in designs that are incorporating a major motif, compose the image (flower, fish, etc.) in the central area so that it can be seen as the focal point. For variation and interest in a design, try placing additional motifs so they "bleed" off or go beyond the borders of the design.

A border can be incorporated into the painted design or it can be added as a flange during the construction of the pillow. As a designer, I find that developing original borders, both on scarves and pillows, is one of my favorite challenges. A border not only serves to highlight the composition but can also be an integral part of the design.

PILLOW. © Linda France Hartge and David Hartge. *To frame and enhance the images, borders were created with strips of colored fabric.*

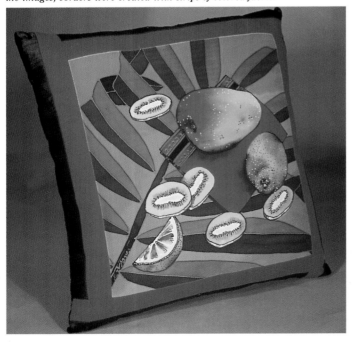

QUILTED PILLOWS

Quilting on a pillow cover adds extra visual and tactile dimensions to the design and the creative options are endless. To help you get started, here are a few suggestions. First, decide if you want to make a whole-cloth quilt cover or a pieced pillow cover. If you decide to piece, for tactile interest, try combining some of the many beautiful silk weaves available in various finishes and textures. If you choose to design and paint a whole-cloth cover, you might consider quilting by following the lines around the shapes that you made with the resist. The stitching will add form to the already painted motifs.

When planning your painting, you will need to take your resist into consideration. Some resists, like solvent-based gutta and wax, will need to be removed from the silk prior to quilting. Other resists, in the decorative category, that remain in the fabric, should be tested to make sure they will not gum up your sewing machine and needle when stitched over.

Preparing the Silk for Quilting

It is very important to make sure that all the fabrics that you plan to use in the construction of a quilted pillow cover will not shrink or are preshrunk. Preshrinking helps ensure that once sewn together, the fabrics will not pucker due to uneven shrinkage during a future washing or dry cleaning.

Even though your painted silk will not need preshrinking, it may need to be ironed before quilting to remove any wrinkles. To do this, cover the silk with a press cloth (silk organza)to protect it and iron, using a steam setting. As you construct your pillow, continue to use the pressing cloth when ironing your work.

Construction

To construct a pillow, outside of the usual machine sewing supplies, you not only need to consider the many silks but also the interfacing, batting, backing fabric, thread and needles, and pillow stuffing you are going to need and use.

When quilting with a slippery fabric such as silk that easily looses its shape, you can stabilize the silk by backing it with a lightweight fusible interfacing. My favorite is French Fuse, which is a stretchy synthetic fabric that has an adhesive on one side so you can attach it easily to the back of your silk. It provides body and stability, and the silk remains soft and pliable. To help make the cutting easy and exact, bond the fusible to the silk first and then use a sharp pair of scissors or a rotary cutter on a rotary cutting mat to cut your pieces.

Quilted pillows get their three-dimensional look from battings, which is quilted onto the back of the painted silk. Batting come in many different fiber contents—for example, polyester, cotton, wool and silk. A selection of batting is sold in many fabric stores that cater to quilters. The batting is available in low-loft (thin) or high-loft (thick) and a variety of thicknesses in between. When machine quilting, if you use a low-loft batting, it will provide a subtle three-dimensional effect and is easy to work with. Several different types of low-loft batting are used in many Art Quilts. The high-loft is a challenge to work with but the effect can create a luxurious bed quilt with coordinating pillows. If you do not want to get involved with the actual quilting, have a professional do the hand or machine quilting for you. They can also help direct you on your choice of batting, thread and backing fabrics. Just make sure that they know how to work with silk and have

MALE AND FEMALE PILLOWS. © Kathy Ciocci and Alexis Ka. *This whimsical duo is set off by borders that are painted as part of the design. The borders hold the eye within the composition, and the colors provide bright accents for home decor.*

them construct a sample with the chosen materials and your silk before they proceed. A professional quilter can be located in the ad sections of quilters' magazines.

Most quilts require a backing fabric partly to support the batting and also because the back of the quilt will be seen. If your pillow cover batting needs support or if the fibers might catch on your machine, you will need a backing. This can be a thin piece of cotton or cotton polyester.

To proceed with the construction, lay the batting between your finished silk fabric, now pieced or whole-cloth, and the backing fabric. Tack the layers together with large basting stitches to hold the layers from crawling and puckering during the quilting process. Once basted, machine quilt the layers, following your design using a free-motion quilting technique, where you are moving the fabric freely in any direction to follow the shapes in your composition rather than quilting in a straight line. Use a special open-toed embroidery presser foot. Like a regular sewing machine presser foot, the open-toed foot holds the fabric down and in position while you are stitching. But, because there is no bar between the toes, it doesn't block your view of the stitching and will allow you to see and follow your resist lines better.

To turn and move the fabric easily while stitching, discharge (remove or drop) the feed dog. The feed dog is the ridged gear below the presser foot that helps move the fabric forward through the machine as you stitch. You usually place your fabric over this and under the foot and machine needle. The feed dog rotates, and as it turns, the friction from the ridges pushes the fabric straight ahead under the needle. In free-motion quilting, it is better to remove or lower the feed dog to facilitate moving the fabric in other directions. If this is not possible, cut a piece of heavyweight paper approximately 2 by 3½ inches and tape it down over the feed dog.

After you have finished applying the quilting stitches, sew the back of the pillow to the front as you would with a plain pillow, leaving a section of one side unsewn to allow for stuffing. After inserting the filling, close the seam with a simple slip stitch.

Needles and Thread

When sewing with silk, use a new, sharp needle designed specifically for woven fabrics (suggestion: 80/12 or 70/10 Schmetz Universal). Test the needle by stitching a practice piece of silk (complete with interfacing) over the batting. If the needle is creating pulls, switch to a new one or try a needle with a finer point. Purchase extra needles and remember to change them often. In general, it is best to use a new needle for each project. If the thread breaks and frays during stitching and you have already checked and adjusted the tension on your machine, this may be an indication that your needle is too small for the thread. Switch to a larger needle. On the other hand, if the needle is too big for the thread, the tension of the stitches will be uneven. In this case, switch to a smaller needle. Again, make a few tests first to ensure the best results.

When it comes to decorative thread, there is a world of choices that will add another texture and dimension to your work.

MOUNTAIN PEONY. © Susan Louise Moyer and Venera Hoerrmann. *Since a decorative resist may clog your machine, you may need to hand-quilt a design executed with a resist that will not be removed from the silk, such as the black gutta used on this pillow.*

SHELL PILLOW. © Susan Louise Moyer. *An interesting and integrated design effect is created on this machine-quilted pillow by letting the center image overlap with the border.*

If you plan to quilt following the resist line, the color of the thread can be chosen to coordinate or contrast with your gutta line, or it can be invisible. Purchase quality thread and be aware that some of the decorative threads work best with a specific needle, so you may need to inquire and do some hands on research.

Pillow Stuffing

As mentioned before, once stuffed, the pillow will have shape, and this often affects the composition. As you become more experienced, you will be better able to anticipate the pillow shape and adjust your designs as you are creating them. Pillows can be stuffed with either a loose synthetic-fiber filling or a preshaped pillow form. I find that my pieced and quilted pillows look better if I stuff them with loose synthetic fiber fill and not a pillow form. The pillow will lay flatter with less distortion showing off the design. When using loose filling, make sure you pack it evenly inside the cover so that the pillow is not lumpy. If using a pillow form, choose one that measures at least 1 to 2 inches larger than the actual cover so that the pillow is full and firm. This is especially effective for whole-cloth quilts when you have quilted the pillows by following the resist lines. A firmly and fully stuffed pillow will stretch the cover and show off the quilting shapes.

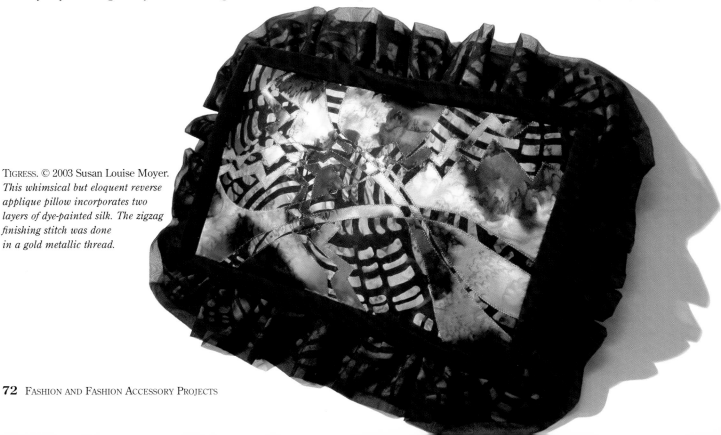

TIGRESS. © 2003 Susan Louise Moyer. *This whimsical but eloquent reverse applique pillow incorporates two layers of dye-painted silk. The zigzag finishing stitch was done in a gold metallic thread.*

APPLIQUÉS

Appliqués are pieces of fabric cut out and sewn onto garments, fashion accessories, pillow covers, wall hangings, quilts, and any other fabric background surfaces. They can be preplanned and painted to incorporate specific creative and visually interesting abstract and representational design elements into a project. Appliqués also provide an opportunity to work with various fabric textures; for example, silk appliquéd over linen can create a very rich look. Pieces of your painted silk, which might even be odds and ends left over from previous creations, can also be successfully spot placed and appliquéd onto silks and other natural fabrics to add a creative spark to any project. The three kinds of appliqué techniques discussed here are machine-stitched decorative edged appliqué; appliqué with the edges turned under and attached with a blind hem stitch or zigzag either by hand or machine; and reverse appliqué which is cutting away shapes to reveal the fabric beneath.

Choosing and Stabilizing Appliqué Fabric

Silk appliqué pieces can be stabilized so they retain their shape and are easier to handle while being stitched. If you sew a light-colored appliqué piece onto a darker ground, the underlying color may show through. Backing the silk with a white fusing material will make your appliqué more opaque and help to eliminate the dark shadows.

For machine-edged appliqués where the stitching is part of the design, a stabilizing material is attached to the back of the silk prior to cutting out the actual appliqué shapes. This stabilizer has a light adhesive on both sides and is often referred to as a paper-backed fusible web. This adhesive enables you to tack down your appliqué pieces so that they don't shift around as you secure them with the decorative stitching.

There are several stabilizing products on the market. They vary in stiffness and involve various methods of application, so you will need to experiment to find the appropriate brand for your fabric's weight and hand, and then follow the accompanying instructions carefully. Keep in mind that the fusing materials used for appliqués on garments should not be so thick or stiff that they disrupt the drape of the garment fabric.

When working with very lightweight and sheer silk, try using the water-soluble stabilizers. This type of stabilizer is basically used to make handling and stitching the silk fabric easier. The water-soluble stabilizers do not hold the appliqué in place on the ground fabric. For this purpose there are spray adhesives that will spray-baste the appliqué in place. Once the appliqué is applied to the ground fabric, the stabilizer is washed out and the fabric regains its natural drape and sheerness.

If you plan to turn under the edges of a shape and hand or machine appliqué so that you do not see the stitches, the following method will create a neatly-turned edge. If needed, the silk can be fused first with French Fuse. Then cut out the silk appliqué shape ¼ inch larger all around than the finished shape. Next cut out a template of the finished shape in a lightweight cardboard. Center the template on the back side of the silk appliqué and lay flat with the template facing up. Cover and protect your ironing board with a clean white sheet or a similar

SEATTLE EXPERIENCE. © Susan Louise Moyer. Pillow construction by Debra Jeanne Reddig, DeGray Designs. *I used the Japanese roketsu-zome wax resist technique (discussed further in chapter 7) to execute this design. After applying Wonder-Under stabilizer to the back of the silk, I then cut the design out of the fabric and used it as an appliqué. For the pillow, Debra (the seamstress) chose textured silk fabrics that would coordinate with the colors found in the shell.*

SARAH'S LILY. © Susan Louise Moyer. *This floral appliqué is made from one of many demonstration pieces that I have executed for my workshops. The overalls, a purchased garment, were washed and ironed before the silk appliqué was sewn to the garment. After applying Wonder-Under, I carefully cut out the design and then it was satin-stitched to the bib.*

white fabric. Spray some starch (Niagara Spray Starch) onto a small piece of clean terry towel and dab it onto the ¼ inch back edges of the silk appliqué. Use a steam iron to turn and press the silk edges over the template. As you work around the shape, clip points and curves as needed. Make sure the spray starch is dry so you do not lose the crisp edge. Remove the template and turn the silk shape over to the right side and you are ready to hand or machine appliqué.

If you are preparing several appliqués, avoid a build-up of starch on the ironing surface. The starch will scorch, turning a yellow-brown which may stain your silk. So constantly move to a clean area on the white cloth.

Satin Stitching

There are several types of decorative stitches you can use to permanently sew down the appliqué shapes. The most versatile and useful one is the satin stitch, in which the thread is sewn back and forth over a fabric edge. It easily echoes or follows the outline of the appliqué, while creating an additional design element, and it covers and therefore finishes the cut edges of the appliqué pieces as it attaches them to the ground fabric.

To execute a satin stitch, your sewing machine must have a variable zigzag-stitch feature. It allows you to choose the stitch width and length that will work best with your design and your fabrics, and most contemporary machines have it. The satin stitch is a tight, more closed version of the zigzag stitch. To switch the machine from a zigzag stitch mode to the satin stitch, shorten the length of your stitches. The width of the satin stitch,

in relation to that of any resist lines, is an important consideration. If you are stitching over the resist lines, the widths of the stitches and the lines should match so that the thread just covers the line. Note, too, that any stitching on finer fabrics will lie flatter and look better with a narrow satin stitch of about ¹⁄₁₆ to ⅛ inch, while heavier fabrics with more body and texture can support a slightly wider stitch.

Needle size and thread are major considerations when executing a satin stitch. Try a size 9 U.S. (65 European) or 10 U.S. (70 European) universal needle and a fine machine-embroidery thread. Test your needle, thread, and fabric combination and practice your stitching before starting. You should also use an open-toed presser foot, preferably one that has a wide, flanged channel on the bottom. The channel allows the raised satin stitch to pass under the foot without getting caught, and the flanged (slightly curved) edges of the channel provide flexibility in turning so you can maneuver around tight curves. Keep in mind that the stitches should interlock on the underside of the fabric so that the bobbin thread does not show on the top of the appliqué.

Frequently, when you are satin stitching your appliqués, you may need to change directions. The best advice I can give for handling this is to stop the machine and pivot the silk. Leave the needle in the fabric, raise the foot, and turn the fabric; once you have positioned the fabric as you need it, put the foot down and continue sewing. For outside curves, stop the needle as it enters the *garment* fabric, and then pivot. For inside curves, stop when the needle enters the *appliqué* fabric and then pivot. If your stitches slant at awkward or uneven angles and become difficult to control, you are not pivoting enough. If your shapes have sharp corners, you can either overlap the stitches or butt them up against each other. Either way, pivot when the needle is in the *garment*, not the appliqué. For soft curves, you will not need to pivot. Just carefully follow the form. Practice your satin stitch until you understand when to pivot so as to avoid unsightly gaps on your actual project.

In order to satin stitch a silk appliqué to another fabric, you may need to use a background stabilizer to prevent tunneling (ridges that occur when stitches are sewn too tightly), puckering, and shifting. The stabilizer is placed underneath the background fabric, to which it becomes attached as you sew on the appliqués; later it is simply torn away. A background stabilizer can be a sheet of tissue paper or a slightly heavier paper like newsprint; other options include ordinary plastic freezer paper or Tear-Away Soft, which works well on fine, silky background fabrics.

Thread Color

The choice thread color is another creative decision. As you make your choice, the following are a few pros and cons that you might want to take into consideration. If you are sewing along resist lines, a thread that blends well with the color of those lines adds texture but does not change the original color or design. Another very effective option is to coordinate the appliqué thread with the garment fabric color and the appliqué. The matching thread visually integrates the background with the appliqué. A thread color that contrasts with both the ground and the appliqué will become a strong design element, but may detract

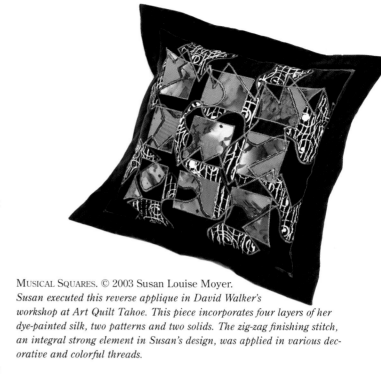

MUSICAL SQUARES. © 2003 Susan Louise Moyer. *Susan executed this reverse applique in David Walker's workshop at Art Quilt Tahoe. This piece incorporates four layers of her dye-painted silk, two patterns and two solids. The zig-zag finishing stitch, an integral strong element in Susan's design, was applied in various decorative and colorful threads.*

from the appearance of the appliqué itself. A thread that only coordinates with the background fabric, and not the appliqué, is something else to consider, but it will make the appliqué shape seem smaller. A dark thread stitched over a light ground or vice-versa is still another alternative, but it will look messy if your stitching isn't perfect.

To apply an appliqué with a turned hem and for piecing, I use invisible thread and the blind-hem stitch or narrow and long zigzag stitch on my sewing machine. Invisible thread is a clear, lightweight, nylon thread which doesn't detract from the color of the fabric.

Reverse Appliqué

The technique, REVERSE APPLIQUÉ opens up a whole new array of design possibilities. A simple but beautiful design can be made with one salt-textured piece of silk and one solid color. The solid color could be painted on a textured weave or it could be a piece of linen. For ease of handling, start by backing your silk with French Fuse. Then baste the two layers of fabric together. Develop a design with strong positive and negative shapes. Draw your design on the back of your basted layers. Sew a straight stitch along all the lines of your design. Turn over and mark the areas to be cut out on the front. Cutting from the front side, use sharp appliqué scissors to cut away every other shape or whichever shapes you desire to reveal the design. Cut close but carefully alongside the straight stitch. Choose a decorative thread and finish the appliqué with a zigzag stitch over the stright stitch. The width of the zigzag stitch should cover the edges where you have cut the appliqué.

SILK APPLIQUÉ JACKET (appliqué detail). © 1995 Susan K. Tenebruso. *In this detail, the width of the satin stitch matches that of the narrow resist lines. The thread color blends in with the colors of the appliqué fabric and the textured natural silk fabric. Therefore, the stitching does not detract from the subtle and delicate design.*

HANDPAINTED SILK TIES. *These ties utilize nondirectional and two-directional designs. The tie at left was created by Susan L. Moyer, the second from left and the last by Christine Mariotti, the center one by Nan Hibma-Doremus, and the rest by Joanell Connolly.. (All designs © the artists.)*

NECKTIES

During the late 1960s and early '70s, I designed and painted men's neckwear. It started with a few ties I painted for my husband, Dale. They became popular among the people he worked with, and I began to take orders. It was my first adventure into the world of business, and I found myself learning the ropes in the New York garment district. By the time this enterprise was in full swing I was filling orders for various boutiques, Saks Fifth Avenue, Neiman Marcus, Paul Stuart, and Barney's, which had just opened its doors.

I learned about proper tie construction from the highly skilled seamstresses at the Countess Mara tie company, and I picked up tips about styling from working with various neckwear buyers and the editors of the menswear magazine of the *New York Times*. The information in this section reflects the most important things I learned from these sources about designing and constructing ties. You should purchase a tie pattern (available at most sewing stores) and familiarize yourself with the included step-by-step construction processes before embarking on a tie project. My guidelines will then serve as helpful hints. If you are planning to have your ties professionally constructed in a factory, request a tie template so that you can determine the placement of your designs, especially if they are to be spot-placed.

TIES. © Louise Blumberg Designs. *The unusual stripes in these fabrics create an interesting variation on the traditional diagonal-stripe tie surface design layout. The resist line is a strong element as well.*

Tie Fabrics and Other Materials

A tie should feel soft but still have enough body to retain its shape. The silk should be at least 14mm and preferably a plain, jacquard, or twill weave. (Twill weaves are distinguished by the pattern of diagonal lines created by the individual fabric threads.) If the fabric is too lightweight it will sag and pucker, and create a wimpy knot and flimsy, curly edge. Tie fabric is cut on the bias, which means it is cut on a diagonal line that is usually at a 45-degree angle to the selvage (the edge of the fabric). Cutting on the bias makes the fabric stretchier because you are cutting diagonally across the grain (the direction of the fabric threads),

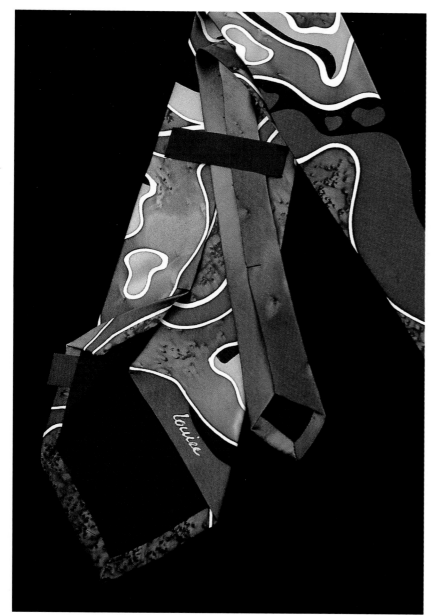

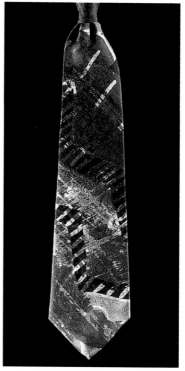

TIE BACK. © Louise Blumberg Designs. *At left is the back of a professionally constructed tie. You can clearly see both the loop (with the narrow end of the tie threaded through it) and bar tack (black stitching near the end of the center seam). Here, the loop was made from a piece of ribbon that was color-coordinated to match the tie fabric. The straight-grain fabric of the lining gives the bias-cut tie fabric shape and a finished look.*

TIE. © 1991 Marcuse. *This two-directional layout makes use of bold color combinations.*

creating more give in the cloth; it therefore falls differently than regularly cut fabric, resulting in a smoother fit and a more flowing line in most garments. A tie that is cut on the bias will lie properly, hanging flat against the body without twisting. If it twists, it was not cut on the true bias (an exact 45-degree angle).

Ties also require interfacing to help maintain their shape. There are two types commonly used in tie construction, both of them relatively lightweight but with high loft (fullness and height). One is a wool or wool/rayon blend and is dry-cleanable; the other is a synthetic. Experts at your local sewing store can help you decide which type is more appropriate for your tie. A lining fabric (usually an opaque silk or silky synthetic) covers the interfacing for a finished look.

Construction

Tie fabric is first painted, then cut, and finally, sewn together. Although there are preconstructed, unpainted tie blanks avail-

able in some craft stores, I strongly advise that you do not use them with the processes presented in this book. Silk fabric preshrinks naturally during the dyeing and setting processes, and since the premade ties are not dyed and steamed, they are not preshrunk. As a result, they become misshapen as they shrink during painting and setting, and ultimately do not lie flat and straight against the body. It is best to paint your own fabric and then construct the tie yourself.

Seams

The main seam on a tie is the center back seam. While hand slip-stitching this, you may have trouble controlling the bias-cut fabric, due to its increased stretchiness. It might help you to cut two forms out of cardboard in the shapes of each end of the tie. Place the fabric around the forms, and use them to hold the shape of the tie while applying the stitching. Remove them only after pressing the seam (see the section below).

Pressing the Tie

Traditionally the edges of a tie, where the fabric folds from the front to the back, are softly curved (or rolled) and should not be pressed flat into a sharp crease. For the well-dressed man, a flat tie is considered a fashion gaffe. So when ironing a tie, place a lightweight, natural-fiber press cloth over it, and hold the steam iron a few inches above. Allow the steam to penetrate through the press cloth for a few seconds without touching the iron to the fabric. Only the v-shaped ends of the tie should be ironed flat.

Loops and Bar Tacks

Another indication of good tie construction and design is the appearance of a fabric loop on the back of the wide end of the tie. This loop holds the narrow end in place while the tie is being worn. You can construct it out of the tie fabric or it can be a piece of ribbon in a coordinating color. The loop is usually placed 6 inches or more above the point and should be as wide as the narrow end plus ⅜ inch. Turn the ends of the loop under ¼ inch and slip-stitch it in place.

And finally, a tie is not complete without bar tacks on the backside of both the wide and narrow ends. The bar tacks are a few handsewn stitches that reinforce the ends of the center seam during the strain of tying and untying the knot.

Design Layouts for Neckties

There are two types of pattern layouts used for cutting tie fabrics. One is a spot-placed method of design in which the motifs are created expressly for the finished shape of the tie. When designing for spot-placed ties, plan for seam allowances, width of tie, and the general placement of the knot versus the design so that your images fall in the intended areas. Note that when worn, a tie should be knotted so the point reaches to the top of the pants waistband.

The more common pattern layout is for ties that are to be cut from fabrics with an allover design that is not necessarily planned specifically for ties. Since all ties are cut on the bias, directional designs like stripes will become diagonal. When painting fabric that will possibly be used for a tie, follow the guidelines for surface design layouts in chapter 4. It might help to make a tie template to check the proposed arrangement of the designs prior to cutting any fabric. Use cardboard or heavyweight paper for the template, and cut the opening to the planned width and length of your knotted tie. When using, remember to place it on top of your silk on the bias, since this is how the fabric will eventually be cut.

EDGE FINISHES

The edges of a fabric, especially those remaining exposed or in view, are important details on any garment or accessory. The Swiss-edge hem, the scarf-edge hem, and lettuce-edge hem are a few easy yet decorative techniques for finishing the edges. These hems are all variations on the adjustable zigzag stitch, so you will need this feature on your sewing machine. You will also need to plan for a ½-inch hem allowance when first cutting your silk. This allowance of fabric is necessary to ensure that your fabric does not tunnel or get jammed in the feed dog. If you did not plan for a seam allowance and are using either the Swiss-edge hem or the scarf-edge hem, you can experiment with substituting tear-away background stabilizers (used with appliqués) for this fabric

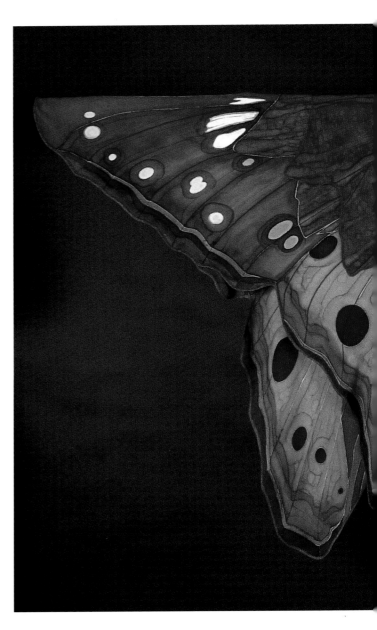

allowance. Place it under the edge of your garment where the allowance would have been and follow the directions below, treating it as you would extra fabric. Note that this technique will work when using a lettuce-edge hem; just stretch the fabric over the stabilizer to achieve the lettuce effect.

Swiss-Edge Hem

This hem edge has a round look to it due to the satin stitching over cord. It is often used as a hem for chiffon dresses.

1. Adjust your machine for 12 to 15 stitches per inch.
2. Sew a regular straight stitch where you want the edge to be.
3. Choose a color-coordinated heavyweight buttonhole twist (a thread used to finish buttonhole edges) or pearl cotton thread and place it over the stitch line.
4. Using the zigzag stitch, stitch over the cording and straight-stitch line.
5. Carefully trim off the seam allowance fabric.
6. With a slightly wider zigzag stitch, sew over this first stitching to finish the edge.

SATYRIDE. © 1994 Judy Barnes Baker. *The delicate veins on this unusual butterfly-wing cape were created by applying alcohol diluent to a dry, painted ground. The diluent lifted and pushed the dye, forming lines of more concentrated color. The edges of the wings were sealed and finished with thinned acrylic medium.*

Scarf-Edge Hem

The scarf-edge hem is comprised of a flat satin stitch. To avoid stretching the fabric, which will cause a rippled edge, firmly push the fabric toward the foot with one hand and guide it out with the other. Practice this first until you can maintain an even speed and are pleased with the results.

1. Sew a straight stitch where you want the edge to be.
2. Next, carefully turn the seam allowance under on that stitch line.
3. With the wrong side up, zigzag or satin stitch over the folded edge.
4. Carefully trim away the extra seam allowance fabric.

Lettuce-Edge Hem

Lettuce edging gets its name from its rippled, curly appearance, which sometimes resembles the edge of a lettuce leaf. It adds a decorative, frilly effect and airy movement to chiffon and other lightweight silks. This edging works best on stretchy fabric, and especially on fabric cut on the bias. The ruffled effect is achieved by taking advantage of the fabric's stretchiness. To execute, follow the directions for the scarf-edge hem, but hold the fabric firmly with both hands and stretch it as you zigzag or satin-stitch along the edge.

Acrylic Edge

When I was in college, I worked as an assistant to the set and costume designer of a summer theater company. We kept the uneven and unhemmed edges of some of our dance costumes from fraying by applying a thinned acrylic/polymer medium to them. To use, apply the medium to the fabric edge with a brush, let it dry thoroughly, and cut through it with sharp scissors to achieve a smooth edge. The edge of the fabric will become slightly darker and stiffer, but it will hold up through rough treatment and multiple dry cleanings and washings. As this sealed edge is somewhat less visually appealing than a stitched one, you may only want to try this method with a colored acrylic-based fabric paint. For a clear seal that makes the fabric edge look slightly darker (as if wet), use acrylic-based fabric paint medium.

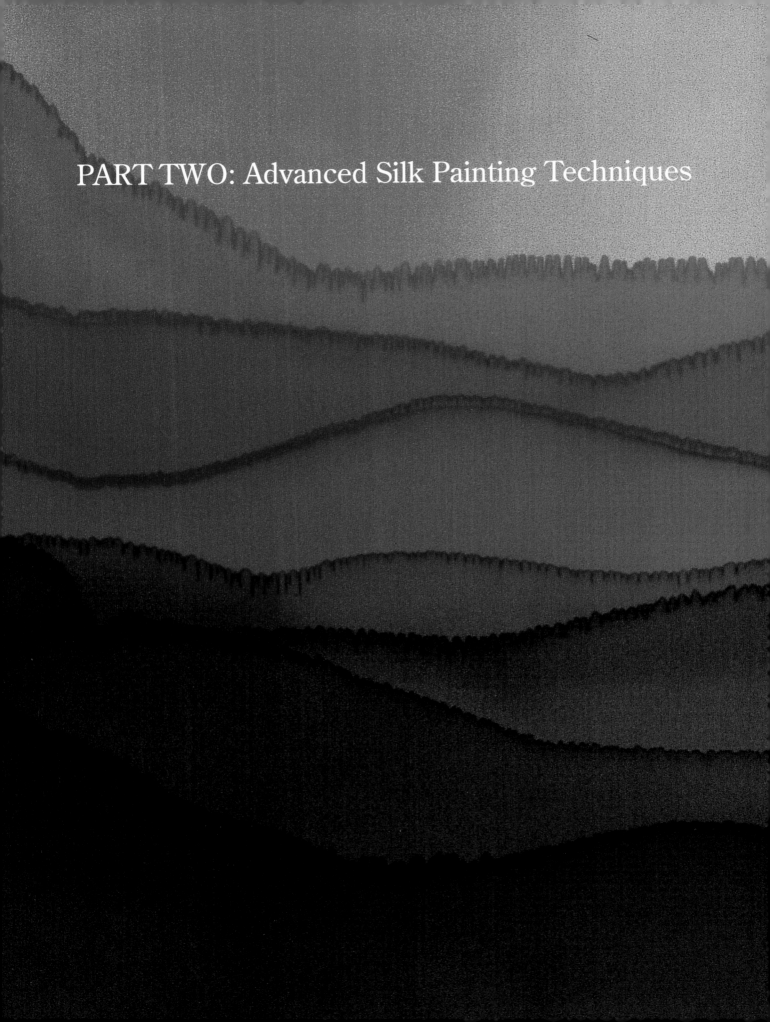

PART TWO: Advanced Silk Painting Techniques

Now that you are familiar with the basic silk painting concepts, you are ready for greater creative challenges. The techniques in the following chapters provide the means to execute more elaborate, complex designs. They combine methods both from other countries and other mediums, and they reveal just how versatile silk painting can be. After you have learned these more advanced approaches, you will be able to express yourself artistically without limitations.

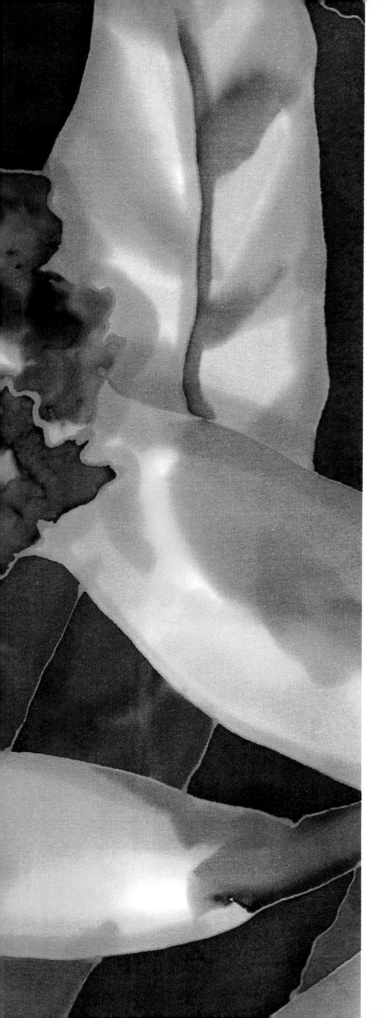

6 LINEAR UNDERPAINTING AND LAYERING TECHNIQUES

For silk painters working in their two-dimensional medium, it is natural to create and layer forms using clearly defined, highly noticeable resist lines. Any shapes are then filled in with color or shading of some sort. There may come a time, however, when you want an alternative technique, one that results in a less linear and more painterly feel. In other words, you may not want such sharp separations between elements in your design, or such obvious outlines. It is at this point that you are ready for linear underpainting.

ORCHID SPORT (detail). © Suzanne Punch

THE LIMITATIONS OF LINEAR RESISTS

Many silk painters who are accustomed to working with other, more traditional painting mediums such as oil and watercolor find that resists applied in a linear manner often restrict their ability to integrate shapes into one another or into the overall composition. This is because the linear function of resist does not lend itself well to blending and shading techniques, and the resulting line cannot be camouflaged. So the resist line not only controls the flow of the dye but becomes a strong (and not always desirable) design element in its own right as well.

In an attempt to make their silk designs more painterly, some artists experiment with tinted resists that they color-coordinate with the dyes in their paintings. However, they soon discover that using a colored resist, which would at first appear to be an ideal solution, does not really solve their problems; the introduction of another color into a painting can sometimes be even more distracting and less integrated than the use of either black or clear linear resists, because this new hue becomes another strong design element.

The Solution: Linear Underpainting

You can resolve this problem by establishing form in your design first with a linear underpainting, which you execute on the silk with dyes of varying color and intensity. This brushwork is then covered (and therefore saved) with clear gutta applied as a linear resist; in this way, the linear underpainting becomes the resist

lines. Due to their colors, which are coordinated with the dyes in the painting, these lines blend with the overall design more successfully than black, clear, or colored resist lines.

Using this technique, you can create a more painterly foundation of many hues from which you can then define and build the forms of your design. The lines become more integrated into the colors and shading of the motifs. Artist Suzanne Punch has eliminated the colored resist lines in her scarves and floral paintings by applying neutral-colored dyes as her linear underpaintings. Once she has applied the resist over those lines, she uses alcohol washes and dyes to obliterate or further soften any unwanted edges of the linear underpainting.

In the demonstration that follows, a linear underpainting serves as a versatile and painterly foundation for defining the form of the images. With this technique, the resist lines begin as simple brushstrokes of color, which are then saved with the overlay of gutta. In this way, the images are freed from being trapped in a hard-edged white, black, or colored resist outline.

Overpainting to Create Form and Depth

Oftentimes, you will want to achieve a true feel of three-dimensional space in your designs. The technique of layering images by overpainting (placing one color on top of another previously applied dye) is also shown in the demonstration. This method creates space and depth in a painting because the darker, overpainted forms recede into the background, pushing the brighter

TOUCANS. © Suzanne Punch. *The linear underpainting on this scarf is used as a strong design element. Its bold color achieves a more decorative approach, in keeping with the spirit of the design.*

areas toward the surface plane and the viewer. *Beetles* (shown below), by professional silk painter Ellen Tobey-Holmes, clearly illustrates this. The images that are closest to us have more detail and vibrant color, while the overpainted images fade into the dark recesses of the painting. This process of successive applications of dye and then resist creates the depth and is referred to as layering.

Layering is not one specific technique but a combination of various aspects of silk painting. Here, Ellen used a linear underpainting at the start of this work, but also incorporated shading, blending, and overpainting methods to create a finished piece.

She also uses the color blue as a common hue to tie the painting together and provide added atmosphere.

Note that the dyes you choose for this technique should move on the silk when nudged with alcohol diluent. As discussed in chapter 1, the dyes that work best for these silk painting techniques are those that do not strike the fabric on contact. In this way, the dye can be easily manipulated and various painterly and textural effects can be achieved. It is also important to work with a gutta rather than a water-based resist, because gutta is much stronger and will better tolerate the alcohol diluent and layerings of color.

BEETLES. © Ellen Tobey-Holmes. *This silk painting was executed with a linear underpainting as a base. Guidelines for using an underpainting to achieve this type of effect are provided in the demonstration that begins on the next page.*

DEMONSTRATION:
Linear Underpainting and Layering

This demonstration piece was executed by Ellen Tobey-Holmes. During my week-long workshop at the Peters Valley Craft Center, Ellen learned the underpainting and dye-layering techniques she illustrates here.

The linear outline of the motif is first drawn on the silk with a blue EZ Wash Out pencil (also available in white for drawing on a colored ground). Used by dressmakers and quilters, these pencils can be found in any fabric shop.

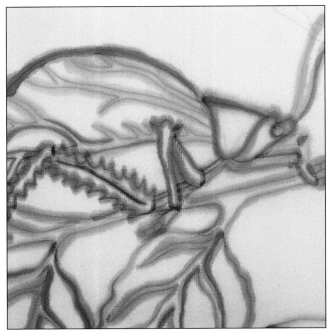

Using a Black Velvet brush, Ellen then applies the linear underpainting of dye over the drawing. Give careful thought to your color choices at this stage, because these hues provide the foundation on which you will build the form in your composition. This foundation will be more effective if the colors of your linear underpainting are shades and tones of those you plan to use in your painting. Brighter colors introduce a strong design element that may be difficult to coordinate and blend with your motifs.

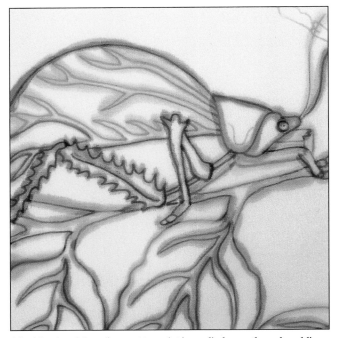

After the dye dries, clear gutta resist is applied over the colored lines of the underpainting. When doing this, it is not necessary to cover the entire width of the lines, which will naturally be broad and uneven; just follow them and apply the gutta in an even manner. Make sure that the gutta penetrates through to the back of the silk; if it does not, it may be that your silk is still damp from the underpainting. (Remember, resists will not penetrate wet silk.) However, if your silk is dry and the gutta still will not penetrate it, thin the gutta down with a few drops of thinner (mineral spirits). Test the new resist mix on a scrap of silk before proceeding.

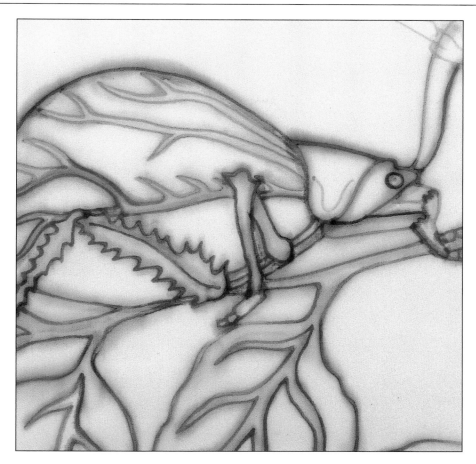

After the gutta is applied, edges of the linear underpainting will remain uncovered on either side of the resist line. Ellen removes or softens these edges with alcohol diluent. To do this, apply the diluent to the outside edges of the underpainting with a brush. The diluent will crawl toward the resist line, dislodging the dye and pushing it up against the gutta line. You can use a small Silverwhite brush to rub the silk and assist the alcohol diluent in loosening the dye. Use a cotton swab to carefully lift and remove the diluent and dislodged dye. Note: It is not critical that all the color be removed; the remaining halo of dye can be worked into your painting and may ultimately make the finished piece more painterly. Ellen has left a bit of a halo here.

Ellen adds the dye to the motifs, and while it is still wet she blends it using a round Black Velvet brush. The delicate details and blending are executed with small, round Silverwhite brushes. The dark dots on the light areas of the bug are made with carefully placed spots of dye. In the darker areas, dots of alcohol diluent are applied to the silk to push the dye away, creating light spots; the result is a ring of dye around a dot of lighter color.

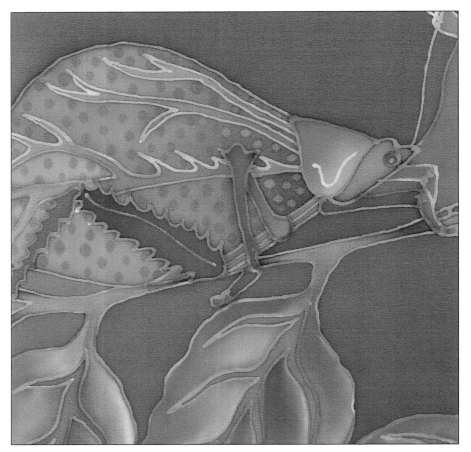

The flat background color is laid down. To avoid streaking when applying a flat ground, work quickly, overlapping the edges of the brushstrokes as you move across and down the silk. It is easy to avoid streaking in smaller areas such as these because the brushstrokes are short. For larger background areas, which are more difficult to paint because the dye dries so quickly, use a background blender or a large, squirrel-hair quill brush (see chapter 1). In either situation, as long as the area is still wet, you can go back over streaks and further dissolve and rub-blend the dye to even it out.

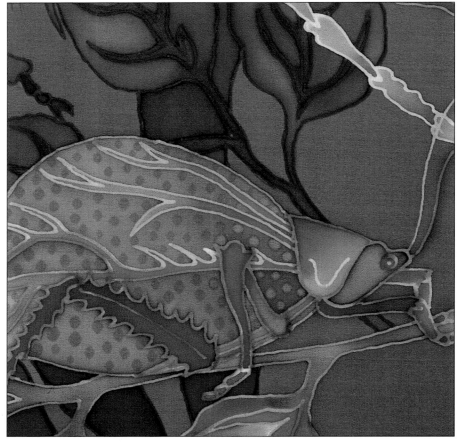

The next two steps illustrate how depth and space can be created in a design by layering images and dye applications. On the painted background, Ellen draws an outline of leaf shapes in gutta. Before applying more dye, Ellen chooses a few leaves that will be lighter than the others and removes some of their background color dye. (For this she uses a small Silverwhite brush and alcohol diluent, which dislodges the dye from the silk; she then picks up the dislodged color with a cotton swab, as recommended in the fourth step.) When first painting over a background color, you may feel as though you are painting in the dark with no guidelines and no definition to the forms, but once the dye dries you will be amazed at the richness and depth of the color. With experience you will be better able to control the color effects.

In the second layering step, Ellen paints another color over the background. She then draws more leaf outlines (over this new color) with gutta resist, filling some in with more dye and leaving others unpainted. She also applies yet another background color to silhouette and really define the unpainted leaves. Notice in the complete painting on page 85, how once the clear gutta is dry-cleaned out, the resist line around the unpainted leaves does not show.

FLOWERS FOR ARLENE. © Susan L. Moyer. *In this commissioned piece, the dyes were mixed to coordinate with the color harmonies and decor of an already furnished room. To give the painting added presence, violet (a color not found in the room) was used to create a split-complementary color scheme involving both the artwork and the room. Several tones of these chosen colors were also applied in the linear underpainting.*

FLOWERS FOR ARLENE (detail of the work in progress). © Susan L. Moyer. *In this sample that I made for teaching purposes, alcohol diluent and a blow drier were used to move dye and create the form of the delicate petals and leaves. The wet diluent lifted and moved the dry dye, creating ridges of concentrated color. Once the ridges were in place, the blow drier was used to dry the silk and further control the flow of dye.*

Hɪʙɪsᴄᴜs. © Merridee Joan Smith. *In this painting, Merridee used the linear underpainting technique to integrate her resist drawing into her painting. By paying attention to color as well as the dark and light areas, she gave her graceful image form. The ripples in the petals were skillfully created by moving the dye on the silk with water and a brush. To hold the ripple effect, as she works, the silk is quickly dried with a hair dryer. She also painted a few of the leaves over the background color. This layering technique makes the leaves recede into the mid-ground, creating atmospheric perspective.*

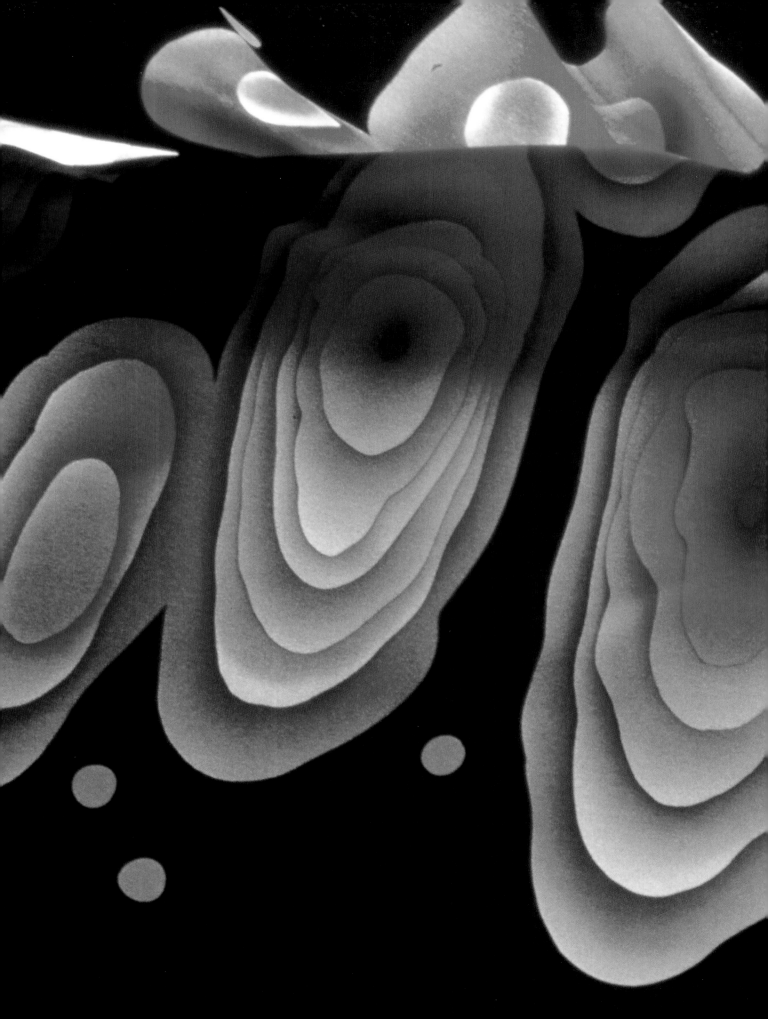

7 WAX RESIST TECHNIQUES

The process of using melted wax and dye for fabric decoration is a technique that predates recorded history. Wax was applied to cloth in order to repel dye, while the unwaxed areas received color by immersion in dye baths. Over time, many different cultures developed their own wax resist techniques, each complete with their own unique tools, wax recipes, dyes, and methods of application. There are the more basic, time-honored batik methods from the island of Java, and there is also the recently re-introduced ancient Japanese *roketsu-zome* technique. While I find it very informative, inspirational, and conducive to my own artistic growth to study and periodically reexamine these various tools, processes, and traditions, in this chapter I will focus primarily on the roketsu-zome method, which can inspire new and diverse techniques and very beautiful results for the silk painter.

UNTITLED (detail). © Ina Kozel.

MATERIALS AND TOOLS FOR WAX RESIST TECHNIQUES

Wax is a highly effective resist material. When melted, it becomes very fluid and easy to apply, and there are many different types. There is also a variety of tools with which to apply wax to silk.

Basic Waxes

Paraffin. This is a white or clear wax that is a petroleum by-product. Its melting point is anywhere between 120°F and 145° F. When applied to silk, it cools to a hard, smooth, clear resist. This even surface makes it easy to see and wipe off any dye residue, if necessary. When cool, it is brittle and cracks easily.

Microcrystalline. Also referred to as micro-wax, this petroleum by-product has a light brown, nutty color and is often used cold by artists for modelmaking and sculpting. It has a melting point of anywhere from 160°F to 180° F, and when applied to the silk, it cools into a flexible resist that won't easily crack. However, unlike paraffin, even when cool it has a slightly sticky surface. This makes it difficult to clean off any unwanted dye residue from the wax. It is also difficult to apply to and remove from fabric. Therefore, it is primarily mixed with other waxes for its flexible, crack-inhibiting qualities.

Beeswax. Beeswax is a natural substance collected from the honeycombs of beehives, which comes in its natural color (yellow) and a bleached version (white). It has a lower melting point (136° F) than microcrystalline wax, but a slightly higher one than paraffin. Both flexible and thick, beeswax does not spread out of control as easily as other waxes. It tends to hold its resist line when applied. Although expensive, many artists use it exclusively because they feel it emits fewer dangerous fumes than the petroleum waxes.

Mokuro. This is a natural, light yellow-green wax from the Japanese haze tree. It has a low melting point and a sticky texture. It is easy to paint with and penetrates the silk well, but on its own it is not a strong resist and so it is usually combined with other more tenacious waxes.

Hakuro. Hakuro is the bleached, slightly harder version of mokuro.

Waxes for Special Effects

Stearin. This is a Chinese wax made from the harder ingredients of the fatty by-products of plants (tallow from the Chinese tallow tree) and animals (both suet and tallow). It is used to create soft, cracked lines.

Wax-balm. Also called carnauba wax, this is a yellow wax from the leaves of the South American carnauba palm tree (*Copernicia cerifera*). This wax is most commonly used as a furniture wax, but in some roketsu-zome techniques it is used to create hard cracked lines that look very fractured. This is done by removing the wax-encrusted silk from its stretcher and crumpling it, cracking the wax.

Ryudo paraffin. This liquid wax can be ordered through most drug stores and chemical supply outlets and is added to other wax formulas to retard cooling and control dripping.

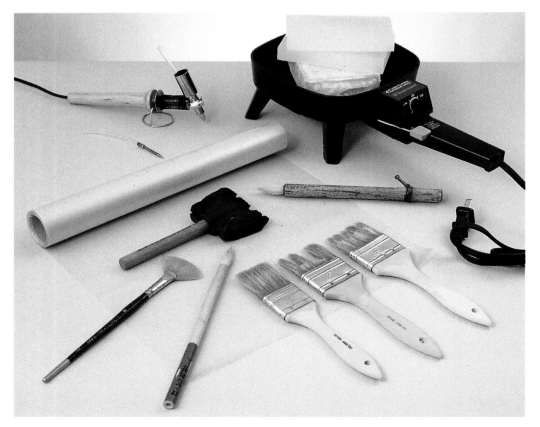

In the foreground are three Silver Econo Gesso brushes, two with their bristles cut and shaped to add special effects and texture. To the left is a Japanese ro-fude brush and a Silverstone fan brush. Above this is a cut sponge brush and one of Keith Lebenzon's handmade bamboo-handle brushes. (Keep hot wax brushes from sticking to a surface by placing them on wax paper as pictured.) At top left is a Rabinowitz Wax Melter Electric Batik Pen. At top right is a Handi-Pan with blocks of beeswax and paraffin.

On the left is a Japanese jizome-bake, made of badger hair, that is used for dyeing large areas and backgrounds; next to it is a peony brush (maru-bake), which is used for shading and blending of dye. These brushes have special handling requirements. Ask for details when purchasing.

Melting Wax

There are many ways to melt wax, but the safest method is to use an electric skillet with a built-in temperature gauge. I use a small Handi-Pan manufactured by Toastmaster. A small pan is stable and easily accommodates any less-expansive work surfaces. Also, with a smaller pan, any brushes that you leave resting on the edges won't slide down into the melted wax. If you are using a larger pan and find that your brushes do slip into the wax, place a clean rock in the bottom of the pan. This will block their fall. You can also cut the bottom out of a shallow can and use the ring for this, too. It is a good idea not to leave your brushes in the wax pot for long periods of time as they can burn and become frizzy.

When working with more than one type of wax, you can heat them all in the same pot while keeping them separate by first placing the individual, unmelted waxes in shallow cans. Put the cans into the pot and begin heating. Once melted, wax should be kept at between 250° F and 260° F. If the wax starts to smoke at all, it is too hot. Check your pot; the temperature control may be defective. When working with melted wax, always ventilate your work area and wear a surgical mask; hot wax often emits strong fumes that can irritate nasal passages.

Brushes and Tools

Wax can be applied to silk in a variety of ways. Traditional processes include using tjanting tools, tjap stamps, and brushes, which have all evolved over time. The tjanting tool is a drawing tool for applying wax in fine lines (as with any linear resist). Hot wax is poured into a metal receptacle and then flows through a spout onto the silk. The spouts are available in different sizes to achieve a variety of wax-line widths. Hand-held electric tjanting tools and Waxmelter Batik Pens are also available; they also create durable, fine wax-resist lines that will withstand repeated applications of diluent and dye. A tjap stamp is a seal made from a heat conducting material that is used to imprint an image in wax on the silk.

Brushes will add a more spontaneous stroke to the wax application. Larger brushes are more appropriate, because they hold more wax and maintain the heat longer in their bristles. You can even cut the bristles of your wax brushes to achieve more unusual designs and textures in your wax application. For example, an uneven bristle edge might allow you to paint an interesting pattern of stripes of wax. The traditional Japanese *ro-fude* brush is a good choice, especially since it has a heat-resistant, bamboo handle. An excellent alternative to this is a plump, round sable watercolor brush that comes to a fine point. Note that most sable watercolor rounds have metal ferrules that will need to be insulated with several layers of masking tape before being used. They become hot very quickly and will burn your hands if left uncovered.

When you are introducing a new natural-hair brush to hot wax, repeatedly dip it into the mixture for a few seconds at a

UNTITLED. © Ina Kozel. *Here, Ina contrasts shape and color to add drama to her wearable art; the juxtaposition of the organic yellow shape against a violet geometric one is very striking.*

These are various sizes of the Japanese brush (bokashi-bake) used for graduated shading and blending of dye.

time, or stroke the new brush with a previously used brush containing hot wax. This will "temper" the brush and help prevent the hairs from curling and becoming brittle. Avoid leaving a ro-fude brush standing in the hot pan. Before allowing the wax to cool, remove your brushes from the wax, stroke them into a point, and let them cool on wax paper.

When choosing a natural-hair brush for wax drawing and masking, look for quality. Select one that gives you excellent control. Although you will need much practice to become skilled at applying wax, a second-rate brush will make wax drawing and masking endlessly difficult.

Of course, you will also need your brushes for dye application, but these should be kept separate from your wax brushes. Do not confuse them. Wax is impossible to remove, so brushes with wax in them are not really cleaned; they are simply allowed to cool and harden. The hard wax in them softens up with the heat of the next application. So your dye brushes should remain exclusively for dyes, and your wax brushes for wax.

Wax Formulas

The following are various wax formulas that silk painter and instructor Betsy Sterling Benjamin uses for the Japanese *roketsu-zome* technique, which is described on the following pages. Since some of the waxes are hard to locate in the U.S., she has also provided alternative mixtures.

Formulas for Traditional Roketsu-Zome

I have provided two versions for each formula, to accommodate varying weather conditions and room temperatures.

		summer hot and humid	winter cold and dry
Formula 1:	mokuro (or hakuro)	70%	60%
	paraffin	30%	40%
Formula 2:	paraffin	70%	40%
	micro-wax	30%	60%
	mokuro (or hakuro)	some	some
	Ryudo paraffin	some	some

For a better, more flexible resist and to prevent the wax application from cracking, add some micro-wax to the first formula. For summer: 58% mokuro/hakuro, 25% paraffin, 17% micro-wax. For winter: 50% mokuro, 33% paraffin, 17% micro-wax.

Alternative Formulas for Roketsu-Zome

These alternate formulas (also from Betsy) are used by silk painters Ina Kozel, Dorte Christjansen, Roberta Glidden, and myself. The first is Ina's standard formula.

Formula 1:	beeswax	50%
	paraffin	50%
Formula 2:	beeswax	80%
	micro-wax or paraffin	20%

Note that the micro-wax will make the second formula thicker, and the paraffin will make it thinner. Also, there are no variations for weather or temperature for these.

ROKETSU-ZOME

When I took part in a workshop at the National Surface Design Conference at the University of Seattle, I was introduced to a Japanese resist technique called *roketsu-zome* by Betsy Sterling Benjamin, a Kyoto-based fiber artist who specializes in this method of applying wax and dye. Betsy has also written a comprehensive book entitled *The World of Rozome: Wax Resist Textiles of Japan,* published by Kodansha International. This informative book teaches the finer points of the traditional Japanese wax resist techniques and beautifully illustrates the history of ro-zome (wax resist techniques) as well as the work of contemporary Japanese roketsu-zome artists.

In this resist process, wax is applied to areas of a design that are to be saved, forming a durable resist. The painting procedure continues with alternating applications of dye and wax. While realizing that I would need years of practice and instruction to become a master roketsu-zome artist like Betsy, my way of thinking about and planning silk paintings was greatly expanded by her teachings.

Wax Application and Brushes

In traditional roketsu-zome methods, which are utilized by the kimono industry, wax is used primarily as a masking agent, much as a frisket is used with airbrush techniques. To mask an area, wax is applied to the silk with a *ro-fude* brush made of sheep hair. It is placed first on the backside of the dry silk (covering any already-painted areas—as with any resist), and then the second and third layers of wax are applied on the front side, over the same spots. More than one layer of wax is used to ensure a strong resist and smooth surface so that dyes do not touch the silk and any excess can be easily and thoroughly wiped off the hard wax surface.

This even wax coverage is maintained by controlling the temperature of the wax (keeping it warm enough to be easily manipulated) and by working quickly to prevent the outside, or leading, edges of wax from becoming cold before the application process is finished. If this process is interrupted and the leading edges harden prematurely, the resist coverage will not penetrate the silk properly and evenly. There may be subtle separations at the points where you stopped and then started the wax application, and the dye will collect in these grooves or recesses. Dye will settle in even the slightest crevices in the wax surface and will ultimately create unwanted textures in the design during the wax removal or steam-fixing process, when the dye becomes deposited on the silk.

Therefore, traditional artists never outline a shape in wax and then fill in the center because the outline may become visible

GAIA SUITE: FERN. © Betsy Sterling Benjamin. *Betsy works in the traditional roketsu-zome and bokashi techniques to create her subtly blended backgrounds. The texture in the ground cloth is rinzu, a satin-faced figured silk cloth. Gold foil threads and chips were added after dyeing using a binder.*

once the dye is applied and seeps into the resulting crack. Instead, the brushstrokes are feathered in from the edge of a form; they are slightly overlapped to ensure that any cooler edges of wax are still warm, melted, and blended together. To apply wax in small areas, use only the tip of the brush; to cover broader areas, utilize the entire brush, including the wider part of the bristles (the belly). When you apply the second layer, place the wax slightly inside the outside edges of the first layer, taking care not to overflow those edges. Successful wax application takes experience but once mastered can lead to a lot of new and exciting techniques.

Dyes and Fabric Sizing

The concentrated liquid dyes that many Japanese roketsu-zome artists use are prepared from acid pre-metallized powdered dyes. Before painting with these dyes, Japanese artists size their fabric with a soybean liquid and water mixture called *gojiru.* American roketsu-zome artists like Bunny Bowen, whose work is featured on the right, have experimented using gojiru with the liquid acid dyes such as Tinfix Design, H.Dupont and Pébéo, and have discovered that gojiru is very beneficial. The gojiru acts as a light sizing, preventing the colors from migrating and streaking excessively, and as it cures on the fabric, its protein content turns into an enzyme that helps bond the acid dyes to the silk. Together with the application of gojiru and the rozome brush technique of working the dye into the fabric, the usual time needed for steam fixation is reduced from three or more hours to one and a half to two hours with little or no runoff.

Before you apply the gojiru, prewash, stretch and dry your silk, soak your brushes in water, and blot with a towel to remove the excess water. Apply only two coats of gojiru (recipe below). The first coat is applied to the silk in a circular motion, overlapping as you go. The second application is applied to crisscross the first application. Do not go back over the application. (Additional coats or a more concentrated soy recipe will create a stop-flow sizing for painting directly on the silk.) Try hard not to make puddles, but if you do, dab them up with a clean towel. Immediately wash the soy out of your brushes so they do not rot.

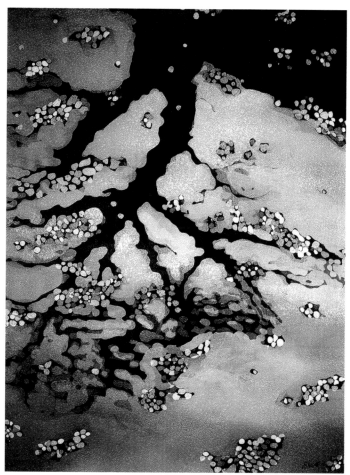

KYOTO SPRING. © 2002 Dorothy "Bunny" Bowen. Rozome on kimono silk, 22″ wide by 28″ tall. *The inspiration for Bunny's painting came while taking a breezy stroll down the Philosopher's Path during the cherry blossom season. "Petals were festooning the dark branches, swirling through the air, piling up in eddies along the path and floating on the canal superimposed on the reflections of the mother trees." It was a magical day for those of us who joined Betsy Sterling Benjamin on a trip to Kyoto. Bunny's painting captures the glory of the day and the poetry of the moment.*

Gojiru Recipe
From the Studio of Betsy Sterling Benjamin

    10 to 15 dry soybeans (found in most grocery stores)

    2-cup container or bowl

    1-2 cups of water

    large bowl

    colander or sieve that fits inside the large bowl

    cheesecloth

    blender

Place the soybeans in the 2-cup container. Cover with water and soak overnight (the water should completely cover the beans). They will expand so make sure your container will accommodate this increase. Drain the beans and then place them and the water in the blender and blend at a high speed.

Place the cheese cloth in the colander and put the colander in the bowl. Pour the soybean mixture into the cheese cloth, gather up the sides of the cloth, and squeeze out the liquid, which is the soy milk, into the bowl and set aside.

Return the soy pulp (left in the cheese cloth) to the blender, add the remaining water, and repeat the process, squeezing the additional soy milk into the bowl. Repeat the process another two or three times, using the strained soy milk as the liquid for grinding.

The soy milk is gojiru. For the techniques of roketsu-zome on silk, the consistency and translucency of the gojiru should match that of thin skim milk. If it looks like whole milk, add more water until you can see your fingers when placed an inch below the surface of the gojiru. Although making fresh soy sizing is preferable, the unused gojiru can be kept in the refrigerator for up to two days.

Dye Application and Brushes

The brushwork technique usually employed in the roketsu-zome method is *bokashi*. It involves the graduated shading and blending of dye in a circular rubbing motion with a dry brush on silk that has been wet with water, and it is synonymous with most types of Japanese dyeing. Bokashi results in deep, rich color, but since the silk is damp, the dyes should be used in a more concentrated form so that the color does not become too diluted and light when it is placed on the saturated fabric.

To apply the dyes in this manner, special, bamboo-handle brushes are used. The *bokashi-bake* is a soft brush with short, dense bristles (badger hair) that have been secured into a full, flat-edged rectangle or round shape similar to that of a stencil brush. It is used for dry-brush blending on a wet ground. The *botan-bake*, or peony brush, is intended for a wetter application of dye because it has a round-shaped edge (rather than a flat, hard one) that prevents uneven applications and streaking. It is also used for shading and blending. The larger *jizomome-bake*, or ground-coloring brush, also has a round edge and is used for backgrounds. I have also found these unique brushes, and the bokashi technique, to be an excellent means of creating areas of blended color (mixing dark to light shades and one color into another) when using other silk painting techniques.

Unfortunately, these hand-crafted Japanese brushes are becoming more difficult to locate because young apprentices are no longer learning the craft of specialty brush making.

Bokashi Dye Application Technique

In the traditional roketsu-zome bokashi technique you work wet-on-wet, applying the dye to dampened silk. Areas of dye that are to be saved are covered with wax, and then concentrated dye is placed on the edges of the wax and blended and graduated on the silk in a circular rubbing motion with a slightly damp bokashi-bake.

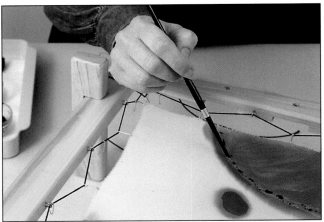

Before any dye is applied, the fabric is treated with gojiru. After this has dried, dampen the silk with water using a sponge. If the painting is in progress and contains areas already painted but not protected with wax, wet the work quickly so the dye won't streak. Begin your painting, let it dry, then cover elements to be saved with wax. After this wax has cooled, wipe it clean and dry. Then place beads of concentrated dye on the wax, near its edges.

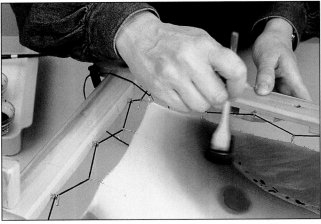

Using a damp bokashi-bake, blend the color into the wet silk to achieve a graduated, dark-to-light effect. Use the circular rubbing motion for this.

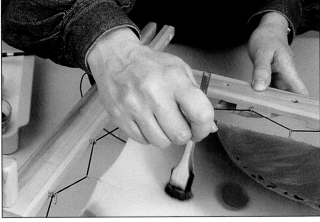

You can obtain a richer color by again placing more dots of dye on the wax edge and blending them into the silk. Avoid streaks of concentrated dye in lighter-colored areas by always blending gradually from dark to light, and blotting the brush on a clean paper towel. After blending, wipe the wax clean of dye. After the silk has dried, apply the wax to new areas you want to save, let it cool, and continue.

Untitled (detail). © Ina Kozel. *Ina worked with the traditional roketsu-zome and bokashi techniques to create the transitions of serene tones accented with bright blue-green dots seen here.*

EXPLORATIONS AND ADAPTATIONS

It takes logic, concentration, and experience to compose and execute wax resist paintings. The numerous applications of dye and wax on the fabric eventually result in multiple layers of form and a strong sense of depth in a composition. Once these skills become internalized, this knowledge will enable faster, more spontaneous expression through the medium of silk painting.

After applying some of the Japanese tools and techniques to my own silk painting, I began to notice how other painters, like Ina Kozel, Roberta Glidden, and Dorte Christjansen, have been directly or indirectly influenced by roketsu-zome. Ina, an artist who studied roketsu-zome in Kyoto and has an extensive background in painting, has developed her own, very untraditional approach to applying wax and dye. She has taken the essence of these techniques—bokashi blending brushwork, and layering of dye and wax to build form—and put them together with an intuitive understanding of her materials. Her wearable art (reproduced on the preceding pages) directly reflects the fluidity of the wax and her medium, and the spontaneous spirit of her involvement with them.

Roberta Glidden, who also attended Betsy Sterling Benjamin's workshop, has been especially diligent about exploring roketsu-zome and has used it to develop her own unique representational style. Focusing her imagery on the plants and landscapes of the West, Roberta finds that through the roketsu-zome process she is able to build more form in her paintings and create a greater sense of depth than with the usual linear resist associated with silk painting techniques (see the demonstration that follows). This method works for her visually, and she also finds the skill, concentration, and practice that the process demands to be particularly rewarding.

Dorte Christjansen, a teacher at California State University, Fullerton, who has a B.A. in drawing and painting and an M.A. in illustration, has been indirectly influenced by roketsu-zome. Her process (also highlighted in a demonstrations in this section) does not embrace the traditional bokashi techniques for shading and blending dye (nor the wax application techniques of roketsu-zome), yet her paintings still reflect the multi-layering of dye that she uses to build form and depth. She applies her wax with round sable watercolor brushes and tjanting tools and applies her dyes with plastic spray bottles, and Black Velvet round brushes mentioned in chapter 1, which she finds excellent for blending. Inspired by the natural beauty of her home state, she finds her garden to be a major source of inspiration and imagery and has compiled sketchbooks full of ideas and compositions. In fact, she treats her garden as a living painting, planting for color and textural variations, which frequently surface in her compositions.

FALLEN LEAVES. © Roberta Glidden. Photo by the artist. *In this surface design, Roberta very effectively creates form and texture. The dry leaf effect was created by brushing in wax leaf outlines and then filling them in with more wax. Applying the wax in this uneven but methodical way catches the dye, creating texture and interest. A tjanting tool was used to suggest veins and highlights on the leaves.*

DEMONSTRATION: Creating a Sense of Depth

A silk painting teacher in the continuing education program at the University of Utah, Roberta Glidden put together this step-by-step demonstration to illustrate how she created her painting *Picked a Pile of Peppers* (right). Drawing on her extensive background in commercial surface design, she covers the basic procedures of how she builds a painting. She uses the natural bleed of dyes applied to wet fabric to add a sense of depth to this piece; when the shape of the motif (here peppers) is then waxed, the bled color remains exposed and is used to suggest shadows.

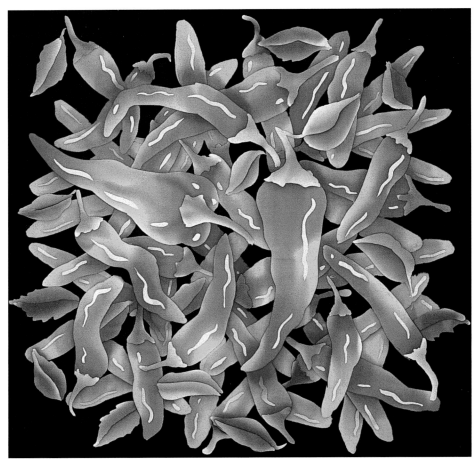

PICKED A PILE OF PEPPERS. © Roberta Glidden. Photo by the artist.

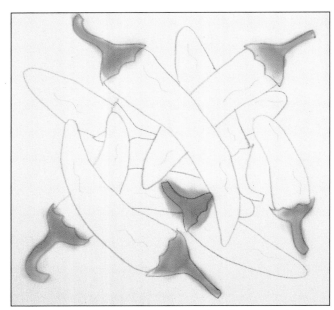

The drawing is traced or drawn on the back of the stretched silk with a soft lead pencil. The frame is then turned over and, with a sponge, the front of the piece is wet evenly with water or alcohol diluent. Once wet, the lines appear clearly on the front side. Working wet-on-wet on the front side, green dye is applied to some of the stem shapes, and the silk is allowed to dry thoroughly. Then the painting is turned to the back side again (where the drawing is still visible) and the green stems are covered with wax.

The front of the silk is again wet with a sponge to make the drawing lines visible. Still on the front and working from the waxed areas outward, gold and yellow dyes are applied and blended on three peppers. The fabric is allowed to dry thoroughly, the painting is again turned to the back, and the peppers are covered with wax. (Note: As the painting progresses, this set of peppers will appear on the top of the pile.)

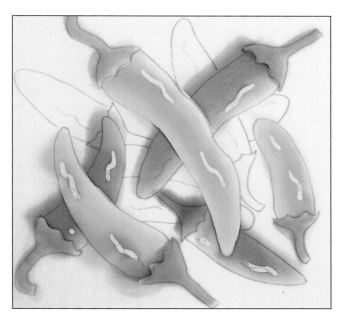

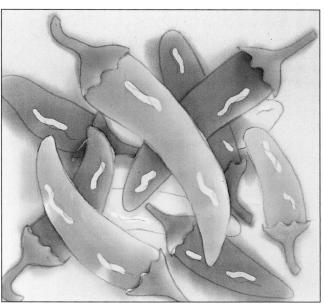

The front is again sponged, and a second layer of pepper shapes are painted using a red-orange color. Again, they are allowed to dry and are then waxed on the back side. (This layer of peppers will appear behind the first.)

Following these procedures, red dye is applied, blended, and shaded on the third layer of peppers, then dried and waxed.

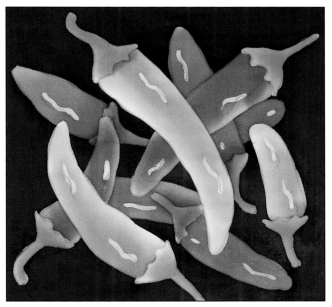

A slightly deeper red is applied, blended, and shaded on the fourth layer of peppers, then dried and waxed.

Finally, the blue background is painted on the unwaxed areas. After the silk dries, Roberta covers the entire piece with wax to prevent migration of the dye during steaming.

DORTE CHRISTJANSEN'S WAX RESIST TECHNIQUE

Through continual exploration of wax resist techniques, Dorte Christjansen has developed a unique approach that involves multiple layerings of wax and dye. For fabric, she prefers a silk with a smooth, even weave that doesn't interfere with her images. The result is a painting style of great beauty, complexity, and subtlety.

Wax Formula and Application

Dorte uses a wax formulated from 50 percent microcrystalline and 50 percent paraffin. When this wax is applied over a color, it creates a muddy, yellow cast, which eventually disappears when the wax is removed from the silk. Dorte suggests painting color swatches of each dye so that you will still be able to make informed color choices when your work becomes covered with and temporarily distorted by the wax. She also suggests that you periodically hold your work-in-progress up to the light to better see underlying colors.

To apply the wax to larger areas, Dorte employs various sable watercolor rounds, which she uses expressly for wax. To ensure that the wax on the brush is always hot enough to deposit a clean stroke and penetrate the silk, she leaves 10 to 12 brushes in the electric wax skillet and rotates their use. She also uses an electric tjanting tool (the Rabinowitz Wax Melter Electric Batik Pen) for outlining and hatching. When working with an electric tjanting, Dorte stresses that to control spills and wax flow, you should fill the tjanting only partway. She also suggests keeping a rag or paper towel handy to hold underneath the tool as you carry it across your work and for any blotting that might be necessary. Of course, you should practice your application technique beforehand as well.

Dyes and Color Palette

Dorte has developed her own basic palette by compiling a variety of compatible silk dyes that she blends to make many beautiful colors. She uses these concentrated stock dyes (concentrated liquid dyes), which are mixed from acid dye powders, and supplements them with compatible H. Dupont, Sennelier, and Pébéo dyes. Her formula for mixing a color from dye powder is as follows: 1 teaspoon dye, 1 teaspoon Calgon (a powdered water softener), 1 tablespoon vinegar, 1 cup boiling hot water. Note that you should place the dye first in only a small amount of the boiling water and then add the remaining water. The Calgon will make the dye move more evenly on the silk.

Dorte's palette consists of these stock colors: canary yellow, turquoise, magenta (a hot pink), vermilion red, maroon (a rich, plummy raspberry), ultramarine, emerald green (a brilliant green), gray blue-green (a teal), red-violet, violet, and black.

Painting Technique

Dorte uses small glass containers to hold her dyes. To them she adds the necessary alcohol diluent to create the desired tints. She uses an assortment of brushes and, when working on large pieces, she often sprays dyes onto the silk with plastic spray bottles. She controls the concentration of the spray both by varying the distance of the spray bottle to the fabric and by working alternately with sprays of dye and alcohol diluent (her diluent mixture is ⅔ alcohol to ⅓ water).

An aggressive painter, Dorte fires away with both hands to

create specked textures, splatters, and gradations. Sometimes she even places the framed silk in a vertical position (as if working upright on an easel), letting the dye drip down the fabric and then rotating the frame so there is a change in the direction of the drips and different colors blend together.

Occasionally, when working with wax resist, spots of dye that are left to dry on the wax may eventually seep through it and stain the fabric, or they may inadvertently dye the silk during any setting processes. This dye will discolor whatever pigment it touches, adding a textural effect that may or may not be desired. If Dorte does not want this effect, she immediately wipes the wet dye off the waxed areas with a damp rag or cotton swab (a technique suggested previously in this section). She also finds that, as her work progresses, the wax resist sometimes breaks down under the repeated applications of dye and alcohol. When this occurs she waits for her painting to dry and touches up the wax application so that it continues to resist the dye.

PRIMAVERA. (detail) © Dorte Christjansen. *Dorte designed this unique, kaleidoscopic arrangement of garden flowers by combining many of her detailed sketches and drawings.*

SUNFLOWERS. (detail). © Dorte Christjansen. *Dorte controls the cracking of the wax application in her complex compositions by rewaxing any areas where the cracking interferes with the design and drawing.*

EPI III. © 1989 Dorte Christjansen. *This floral subject and surrounding border design were executed using Dorte's unique wax resist methods (see following demonstrations).*

CALLA LILY FIELD (detail). © Dorte Christjansen. *Again, Dorte used her drawing skills and her wax resist techniques intuitively to create this spontaneous field of flowers.*

DEMONSTRATION:
Dorte Christjansen's Wax Resist Technique

I asked Dorte to analyze her complex wax resist painting *Calla Lily Field* (a detail of which appears on the preceding page) and explain each technical step and thought process involved in its development. She created this demonstration as a result.

Dorte first draws the outlines of her composition on white paper with a black felt-tipped pen. When she transfers the drawing to silk, this heavy pen line will be easily visible through the silk.

After stretching the silk taut on the Moyer Design Fabric Stretching System, Dorte tapes the paper to the underside of the silk. She places a piece of ½-inch foam board, which fits inside the stretcher, under the stretched silk so that the design is pressed up against the fabric and can be seen through it. Then she traces the design (following these outlines) onto the silk with a regular soft (2B or 4B) pencil. Once finished, she removes the foam board and drawing from the silk and lifts the frame onto its legs so that the fabric is suspended above the work surface for the wax and dye applications.

With her first application of wax onto the unpainted ground, she saves any white areas that she wants to use later as highlights. These highlights will also establish movement in the composition. The linear areas of wax outline the main shapes and thereby control the flow of dye in the painting. At this point, Dorte also puts down her first application of dye (a linear underpainting), and here she uses tints, shades, and diluted washes of various yellow, red, and green hues. While working, Dorte periodically wets the silk with a spray of alcohol diluent.

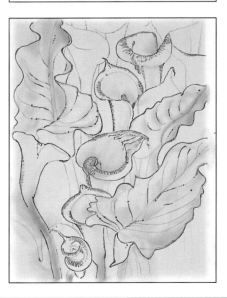

With the second application of wax, Dorte defines the details in the leaves and calla lilies. She does this by drawing a series of linear brushstrokes with the wax (these appear as deep yellow lines because the wax is an unbleached, golden yellow). She concentrates the light effects mainly on the three lilies in the lower left corner of the painting and will later introduce shadows with applications of darker dye. Keeping composition in mind, Dorte has begun to lay the foundation for the diagonal movement, which will be seen in some of the white lilies amongst the darker leaves.

Dorte is now ready for her second application of dye. Dorte keeps the silk moist with an occasional spray of alcohol diluent and, working wet-on-wet (as with the bokashi technique), she intensifies the previously applied greens and yellows by adding more of these hues. She then utilizes a split-complementary color scheme by introducing violet, red-violet, and magenta to the greens. After the dyes are fairly dry, Dorte sprays a light mist of diluted magenta (hot pink) and teal green hues onto the painting to build textural effects. Once the silk is completely dry, additional leaf and stem forms are drawn and saved with wax, creating depth and enriching the background with pattern.

On the third application of wax and dye, Dorte continues building form with layering. She completely covers the top five lilies with wax and fills in most of the leaves, leaving exposed only those areas that are to receive dark accents. To emulate the feeling of depth and sunlight found in her gardens, Dorte contrasts the white of the lilies with darker ultramarine blue and red-violet accents. As the painting dries, she sprays it again with both the diluted teal green hue and the hot pink, occasionally overlapping the applications. To soften the original white highlights on the leaves (saved in the third step), Dorte repeatedly paints dyes over the wax until the color penetrates through to the silk, leaving a slight haze of color on the fabric.

With the second layer of wax, Dorte used hatching and brushwork to define the surface contours of the lilies and leaves. To further define the images, she now fills in the narrow, unwaxed spaces, which outline some of the shapes, with dye. To create more depth in the centers of the lilies, Dorte left them unwaxed and here paints them a deep purple.

Red-violet, violet, and blue-green were applied to the veins of the leaves. Dorte used a very wet brush to apply a color at each end of the leaf vein. The colors flowed between the lines creating gradations where the two colors met. This technique added form to the leaves. Throughout the painting an atmosphere of depth and shadow was created by using blue as a common hue.

To prepare the painting for its fifth and final application of dye (which will be black), Dorte fills in all the remaining shapes and spaces with wax, except for the defining outlines, which she wants to receive the black dye. She also reinforces previously waxed areas with fresh wax or carefully reheats them with the spout of the electric wax tool to seal and bind any cracks or thinner areas. Since the black dye is strong and corrosive, Dorte applies it directly into the unwaxed areas and then immediately wipes it off the wax so that any excess dye does not stain through or eat away at the wax seal. Note that at this stage, the painting appears dull and yellowish from all the layers of wax.

Now Dorte removes the thick layer of wax from the silk. She irons out most of the wax before the painting is steam-fixed. Once the painting is free of the yellow cast of the wax, its true colors are revealed along with all the strong juxtaposition of highlights and dark recesses. Now you can clearly see the diagonal movement and sense of depth created by the contrasting light liles against the darker, receding stems and leaves. The textures created throughout by the layers of hatching and dye convey Dorte's unique style and add interest and form to the images. For instruction on wax removal, refer to the alcohol discharge demonstration on pages 114–115. Directions for steam fixing are provided in chapter 9.

ALCOHOL TECHNIQUES

Used to execute my painting on the cover of this book, the alcohol discharge technique allows color placement effects that would not otherwise be possible. One way to use alcohol (either pure or diluted with water) is to place droplets of it on a painted silk ground. As it spreads into a spot on the fabric, the alcohol pushes the dye to the outer edge of that shape, creating a thin ring of darker color there. When dry, the spot will remain lighter than the ground color and the outer ring at its edge will be slightly darker. Basically, you are using the alcohol to manipulate the dye, and a variety of interesting textures and painterly effects can be achieved. For example, you can apply brushstrokes of alcohol diluent rather than droplets. If you use this method, it is best to let the painted ground dry thoroughly before applying any alcohol, because the effect of moving the color is more pronounced when the dye is dry.

Diluted alcohol can also be applied as a wash to unpainted silk prior to beginning a painting. This wet-on-wet technique causes the subsequently applied dyes to flow and spread more slowly and dry with a softer edge than they would on silk without an alcohol wash. As in the following demonstration, this technique can be combined with wax resist effects to create and integrate contrasting textures into one overall design. The fabric you select for these processes should not be stretchy or have a lot of give. They will stretch out when wet, and as a result the wax resist may crack.

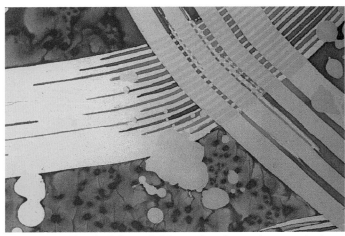

OMBRÉ SCARF (detail). © Susan L. Moyer. *Here, layers of wax caught the loose dye as it was discharged, reflecting the application of one stroke of wax over another. Salt was used to create the textured background effect.*

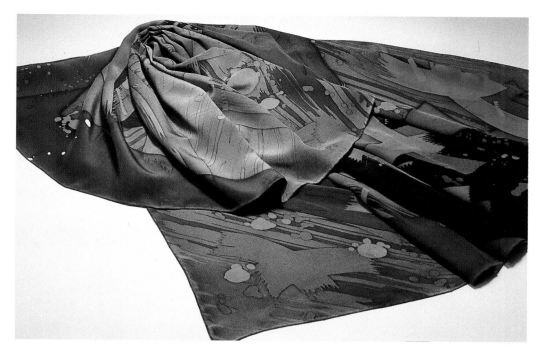

RED BRUSHSTROKE SCARF. © Susan L. Moyer. *Both wax and Sennelier black gutta were used as resists here. The wax brushstrokes were placed over areas of the silk that were dyed red. The black gutta was then applied to section off other areas of color.*

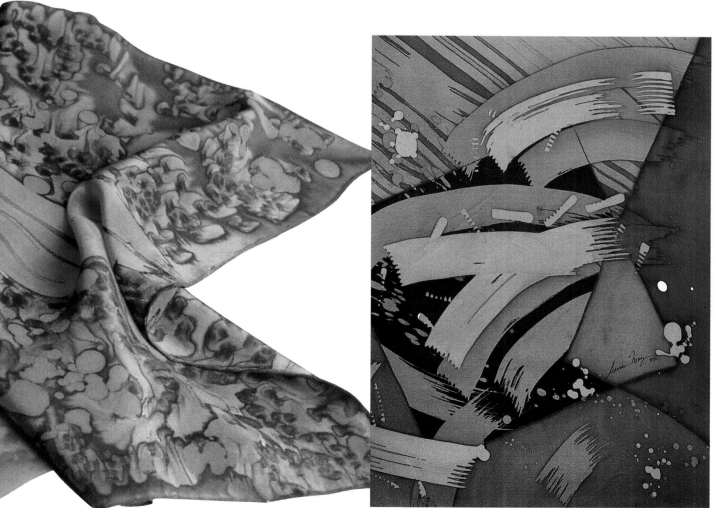

OMBRÉ SCARF. © Susan L. Moyer. *The techniques used here are similar to those explained in the alcohol discharge demonstration on pages 114–115, except that the wax brushstrokes were applied over an ombré ground (a field of continual, solid colors that blend together from light to dark) rather than over separate areas of color.*

RED BRUSHSTROKE SCARF (detail). © Susan L. Moyer. *Between applications of wax, alcohol diluent was used to move the dye, creating drop-shadow effects.*

DEMONSTRATION:
Alcohol Discharge and Wax Resist Techniques

Alcohol helps make acid dyes very versatile and it can provide interesting and unusual effects, but you should remember to work in a well ventilated area with an exhaust fan when using it. The fumes can be overwhelming and dangerous.

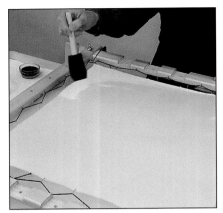

To prepare the silk for the wet-on-wet technique illustrated here, stretch it tautly above your work surface, which should be protected with a plastic covering. Apply a diluent solution (of 50 percent water and 50 percent isopropyl alcohol) to the silk with a foam sponge brush. Don't overwet the fabric and create puddles though, because the dye will run into these spots and spread out of control. Blot the puddles and silk with paper towels before applying any dye.

In this photograph, dye is applied to the wet silk with an oval wash brush. Due to the alcohol diluent on the fabric, the shapes of color spread slowly, drying with a soft (rather than a sharp) edge.

While the silk is drying, melt the wax at 260°F. A mixture of 50 percent beeswax and 50 percent paraffin was used here. Temper the brushes in the melted wax, and execute a few practice strokes on newspaper. (Note: You will need a slightly lighter hand to get the same effect on silk.) Once the silk is dry, apply the wax over the color to be saved. Return the brush to the pan often to keep the wax on it hot and flowing; this will ensure that the wax penetrates the silk properly. (It should look shiny and clear, not dull and chalky.)

Now any dye that is not covered with wax is flushed (or discharged) out of the silk with alcohol diluent and a sponge brush. Place absorbent newspaper under the stretcher frame. Liberally apply the diluent to the fabric and dislodge the color by rubbing the silk with the tip of the brush. Flush the diluent and discharged dye from the silk in a circular motion, add more diluent, and repeat the process. Repeat until there is only a light halo of color left. This may take 8 to 16 ounces of diluent. (I used 8 ounces on the demonstration piece.) Remove the diluent-soaked newspaper, and let the silk dry until it is just damp.

Here dye is applied around the areas of wax resist using an absorbent oval wash brush that holds a lot of dye and comes to a good point (a squirrel-hair quill is another good choice). Overlap and blend areas of color as you do this, but be careful not to leave spots of dye on the wax. For this project, I also made use of the salt technique in which coarse, sea salt crystals are placed on top of the wet dye. The salt pulls the wet dye in various directions, creating a texture on the silk.

Drops of color that have formed on the wax can be removed with a damp cotton swab. Keep in mind that if they are not removed, they may penetrate the silk when the wax is ironed out or the dyes are steam-set.

Allow the silk to dry, and remove and discard the salt crystals. Excessive amounts of salt may attract moisture during the steaming process, causing water spots. Therefore, it is important to scrape off any salt residue that is visible to the eye.

I used both a foam brush and a Silver Econo gesso brush to apply the next layer of wax. I cut grooves into the ends of the foam to create the striped effect you see here. The foam holds a good amount of wax, enabling the application of long stripes, and the altered gesso brush creates the texture and feel of a light, dry brushstroke.

Another layer of dye (here, black) is now applied over the salt-textured ground colors. To obtain a rich black, allow the first application of dye to dry and then add a second coat.

When the painting is finished, all the wax must be removed from it. After the silk is dry, place it on a few layers of clean newsprint paper (approximately ¼-inch thick). Place two more sheets of clean newsprint paper on top of the painting. Using a hot iron on a dry setting, melt the wax into the paper.

Once the newsprint is saturated with wax, place the painting on fresh paper and repeat the process until only a light residue of wax is left in the painting. The painting is now ready for steam-fixing and dry cleaning (see chapter 9). Artists often bypass the ironing step because the wax can be removed during the steaming process; the wax melts off the fabric due to the steam heat.

8 SCREEN PRINTING

As you improve and grow as a silk painter, it becomes a challenge to discover new ways to express yourself. Professional artists often explore other surface design techniques and develop ways to make them compatible with the basic silk painting materials and techniques with which they are already familiar. One such artistic medium is screen printing, a process of making a print by pushing pigment through a stencil (or mask of some sort) and a fabric screen, resulting in an image on an underlying surface. Dye that has been thickened to a print paste consistency, as well as gutta and some water-based and water-soluble resists, can be screen printed onto silk.

My intent is to introduce the silk painter to a few basic screen printing processes that are compatible with the silk painting medium. Although the techniques covered should open the door to a wealth of creative possibilities, it is important to know that there are many more processes and technical aspects of screen printing that are beyond the scope of this book.

UNTITLED. © Kerr Grabowski

117

SCREENS

Screen printing processes, also referred to as silk screen (traditional screens were made with silk fabric), are used for many things. Images are screened onto T-shirts in mass quantities, but artists, perhaps most notably Andy Warhol, also use silk screen to create one-of-a-kind or limited-edition-series works of art. Warhol's silk-screened images of Campbell's soup cans and Marilyn Monroe are familiar to almost everyone.

This versatility provides many options: you can create a single print; a series of multiple, virtually identical images; or a series of similar images with slight alterations—a change in color, perhaps. The artist Kerr Grabowski, whose work is featured here, is constantly exploring the potential of the silk painting medium in relation to her own creative growth. For Kerr, as for all artists, the exploration of this intrinsic relationship is an informative and ever-challenging process. She uses screen printing in combination with other surface design techniques to create her unique fabrics and was very instrumental in assisting me in my experimentation with her screen printing techniques.

Fabrics

Multifilament polyester and less-expensive polyester curtain-sheer fabrics (in white) found at fabric stores and outlets make ideal screens when printing with water-based mediums. Finesse and Ninnon are brands of curtain-sheer fabrics that you might want to try. Multifilament fabrics are identified by a double-X system and range from 6XX (approximately 86 threads per inch) to 16XX (approximately 232 threads per inch). The fewer the number of threads per inch, the larger the openings between the fibers to allow the print medium (the pigment or resist used) to pass through. When using a water-based resist as her printing medium, Kerr opts for a 8XX or 10XX screen fabric (larger openings);

when using dyes as the medium, she prefers a 10XX or 12XX screen fabric (smaller openings).

When working with photographic stencils and solvent-based (or gutta) mediums (covered later in this chapter), a monofilament polyester fabric is better.

Frames

Frames can be constructed with four wooden bars or supports, which are sometimes referred to as balusters. Use two for length and two for the width. To determine the length of the frame bars, select your print size and add 2½ to 3 inches to both ends of each piece of wood. This extra length is an allowance for the wells. These are the borders of the screen, which are masked with tape to hold the print medium and provide a place to rest the squeegee (where it will not touch the screen) both before and after pulling a print. I recommend a wide well because it will better hold resists or dye mediums and prevent them from spreading onto your screen. This is especially true with gutta resists, which can be very runny. Preassembled frames can be purchased at art supply stores in standard sizes and fabrics. Others can be ordered to custom specifications from mail-order catalogues (see List of Suppliers).

Squeegees

Squeegees are used to force the print medium through the open areas on your screen. They are measured by inch widthwise and are composed of a wooden handle with a rubber blade. To adequately push the medium over the entire screen, the squeegee should extend ½ to 1 inch into the side wells when placed in the frame. The blades are available in various durometers (degrees of hardness), with 45 being extra soft and 80 bone hard. Soft to medium blades are recommended for printing onto

UNTITLED. © Kerr Grabowski. Photo by the artist. *Kerr's sophisticated color harmonies, spontaneous drawing, and sensuous textures are the result of a combination of various surface design techniques. She paints directly on the silk with liquid dyes and screen prints with resists, discharge pastes, and thickened dyes. The concentration of blue, yellow, and red hues contrasted against the black and white panels and borders make this a lively triad color scheme.*

SHARK FIN SOUP (front). © Kerr Grabowski. Photo by the artist. *To create her black-and-white designs, Kerr makes a print paste with sodium alginate (see pages 122–124) for her fiber-reactive dyes and then screen prints the medium using a variety of stencils. Some of the panels of this garment were executed with a wax resist technique and others by painting dye directly onto the silk without use of a resist. The contrasting panels were then sewn together to form unique, wearable art.*

SHARK FIN SOUP (back). © Kerr Grabowski. Photo by the artist. *Kerr used paper, wax, and photostencils to print the various panels. To create the subtle blue checked areas, she printed a thin layer of Inkodye resist on the white silk crepe and then painted on it with fiber-reactive dyes. The dye penetrated the thin layer of resist in varying degrees, creating shadowed images.*

textiles because they conform to the fabric's surface and therefore deposit more print medium on it. Finding the appropriate blade flexibility is usually a matter of experimentation, but a good starting durometer is 60 (a standard, medium weight). To support it so that it will not fall into the print medium, you can attach a dowel to each side of the squeegee (see the squeegee in the following demonstration). Take care not to nick the blade when storing your squeegees; a damaged blade may result in uneven distribution of the print medium on your fabric.

Screen Tape and Varnish

Wooden frames should be protected from moisture, otherwise they will warp. The wood can be carefully coated with polyurethane, and the inner sides and the wells should be covered with tape and sealed with a topcoat of shellac. A new and effective alternative is Screen Tape. It is made of polyester film and is very easy to use, because it doesn't need to be sealed and is easy to clean and apply. For the screen in the screen printing demonstration I covered the supports with duct tape and then used Screen Tape to mask the wells and reinforce the inner sides of the frames.

Print Boards

The silk screen print board is a sturdy, padded, lightweight, and inflexible supporting foundation over which the fabric or surface to be printed on (the print surface) is placed. It ensures an even print surface, resulting in good screen-to-fabric contact and thorough, even coverage of the print medium. Complete guidelines

for constructing your own print board are provided in Joy Stocksdale's book *Polychromatic Screen Printing,* but I've outlined the procedure here as well.

Basically, to build a padded print board you will need ½-inch thick dacron batting, sheets of 12- or 16-gauge plastic, muslin cloth, and the supporting, underlying board. One possible board material is a rigid, lightweight, foil-faced foamboard called Energy Shield, manufactured by Atlas Energy Product. You will also need duct tape and pins. To ensure that the screen maintains even contact with the silk on the print surface (and so that the frame doesn't rock when you pull a print), the minimum measurement for a print board should be 1 inch larger than the outside measurement of the screen frame.

To begin, cut a piece of foamboard to the desired print board size. Also cut a layer of batting to match this size. Place the batting over the foamboard and temporarily tack it in place with the pins; the pins should be positioned at least 1½ inches in from the edge and angled toward the center of the board. Then using the duct tape, attach the edges of the batting to the edges of the foamboard by placing half the width of the tape on the batting and pulling it tightly toward the edges before securing it. Make sure the surface is smooth, and remove the pins.

Now you are ready to cut the plastic. Cut it at least 4 or 5 inches larger than the board dimensions (so that you will be able to wrap it around the edges of both the board and the batting and secure it to the board's underside). Place the board upside down in the center of your cut piece of plastic. Pull the plastic over the back of the board and tack down the center of each edge. Then go back to secure these edges more thoroughly. To avoid ripples as you tape the plastic down, place strips of tape at 6-inch intervals (or less depending on the size of the board) on the edge of the plastic and use them to pull and stretch the plastic from the centers toward the corners so that it is taut and smooth on the print board surface. You should leave the corners for last, cut out any excess plastic (that can cause unwanted lumps), and tape down. Avoid creating any creases in the plastic because they will cause uneven textures in your design when the print medium is applied.

When printing, you will need to stretch a backcloth over the plastic and secure it with tape on the print board. The silk is then stretched onto the backcloth and attached with pins or tape. Traditionally, the backcloth is a piece of muslin, which will absorb the excess print medium as it seeps through the silk when a print is pulled. The backcloth is removed and washed between printings.

Screens, Print Boards, and the Moyer Design Fabric Stretching System
Traditionally, printing surfaces for mass-produced fabrics are large enough to accommodate printing repeats on yardage. A larger surface (such as a 4- by 8-foot Atlas Energy Shield) would also facilitate work on several small pieces of fabric so a series (or edition) of prints could be pulled at one time. For the silk painter who has limited space or who wants to produce monoprints (single, unique prints), print boards and screens can be coordinated in size with the Moyer Design Fabric Stretching System mentioned in Part I.

Once you have stretched your silk on the Moyer Design system, it does not need to be removed and restretched on the print board for use in screen printing, as with other, more conventional stretching methods. The fabric remains stretched on the frame throughout all of the silk painting and screen printing processes. For screening, the frame legs are removed and the frame (with the stretched silk) is placed on the print board and under the screen. The system ultimately saves time and space. If you are planning to do successive prints (a series), you will need to set up a frame for each print. The frames can even be stacked while the silk dries on them.

When using this fabric-stretching system for screens of up to 36 inches square, the print screen and print board should fit inside the inner perimeters of the system's stretcher frame (see the following demonstration). For example, if the inside measurement of the frame is 20½ inches square, the print board and screen should fit inside this length, leaving at least a ½- to 1-inch allowance for the metal loops and elastic that run along the inside of the fabric stretcher frame. The maximum outside measurement of the print screen and print board would then be 20 inches square.

Keep the following print screen frame calculations in mind as an example: A 20-inch-square screen frame constructed from 1-inch supports would include a screen area of 18 square inches. The screen will be further decreased 2½ to 3 inches on each side by the taped well, giving you an open print space of 12 or 13 inches square. Note that larger screens would require wider, 1½-inch supports.

The Moyer Design Fabric Stretching System has been developed to encourage experimentation in design and can be adapted

so several techniques can be combined with screen printing to build up a composite design or monoprint (see following demonstration). However, I should point out that it is not designed for perfect registration (placement) when one stencil design is used repeatedly or is to be printed over another screened design.

When screen printing, you can increase stability and control the registration of the print by constructing a hinge bar on the screen that attaches to the stretcher frame, securing the fabric stretcher and print screen frame together. For the screen used in the following demonstration, the hinge bar is attached to the screen with two 2-inch split pin hinges and ¼-inch machine screws so that the print screen can be easily removed afterward. The depth of the hinge bar should be less than that of the supports so that the screen lies evenly when lowered onto the silk. A print can then be pulled without the screen shifting, affecting the registration.

STENCILS
Stencils function in a similar way to the resists used in other silk painting processes. Wherever the stencil covers the screen, the print medium will not penetrate to the silk below. They can be made from paper, wax, and even photographic and light-sensitive materials. Paper and wax stencils are less permanent, while photographic stencils are durable and fairly permanent once adhered to the screen fabric. For this reason, photostencils may be the better choice for the artist who is producing multiple prints of the same design.

Paper Stencils
Stencils can easily be cut or torn from paper. Freezer paper (used to wrap food for freezer storage) is a heavyweight, white paper similar to parchment, which works especially well because its coating prevents the stencil from becoming saturated with the print medium. You can cut or tear out shapes from a sheet of paper and use them as your stencils, or you can use the piece of paper from which they were cut. Either way, the paper stencil is arranged, coated side up, over the stretched silk, and the print screen is placed over it.

The print medium is poured into the well and is pulled across and through the screen onto the silk below using the squeegee. After the first print is pulled, the wet print medium holds the stencil in place on the screen, providing an opportunity to pull a few more prints. Once finished, remove the stencil and clean the screen before the medium has a chance to dry.

Wax Resist Stencils
Liquid hot wax and wax crayons can be applied directly onto the screen to create stencils. For the hot wax, use a mixture of 50 percent beeswax and 50 percent paraffin. It can be applied using a variety of implements, such as tjanting tools and brushes. Apply melted wax to the front of the screen, which should be raised off the work surface. After applying the wax, check the back side of the screen for wax drips. Any drips must be carefully removed with a blunt knife so that the screen maintains even, unbroken contact with the print surface.

Wax rubbings and drawings made on the screen with pieces of wax or wax crayons also make effective stencils. Choose a lightly colored crayon (rather than white) so that you can see it better against the screen fabric. Rub the crayon (or wax) into the

SQUARE SCARF. © Sally Jones. *For this and other scarves, Sally works on a beautiful, heavyweight silk charmeuse. To create her fabric designs, she screen prints thickened dyes and discharge pastes over painted grounds.*

screen until the fibers are filled with wax. To set the wax in the screen, hold a dry, hot iron a few inches above the screen until the wax softens into the screen fibers. Don't heat the wax too much or it will melt through the screen fabric and not be an effective resist.

To clean a screen and wax stencil without removing the stencil, flush it with plenty of cold water. Avoid solvents, which will dissolve the wax, and hot water, which will melt it. To remove the stencil from the screen, place newspaper both on top of and underneath the screen. Iron over this with a warm (not hot) iron until the wax melts out of the screen. The newspaper will absorb the wax and help protect the polyester screen fabric from the direct heat. After ironing, remove any wax residue that may be left by rubbing the screen with a soft rag and a solvent, like Turpenoid or mineral spirits.

Photostencils and Thermal Screen Stencils

Photographic stencils are durable and stand up well to repeated use. Also called photostencils, they are made by placing light-sensitive film material against the screen fabric and exposing it to ultraviolet light. The light-sensitive film hardens on the screen creating a stencil.

The equipment and space (a darkroom is best) required for making these stencils is too extensive to cover in this book. But, you can have photo screens made at professional photo screen suppliers. Make sure you tell them which print medium you plan to use so that they use the appropriate film; water-based print mediums (such as the thickened dyes and H. Dupont Serti HPNO, discussed in the next section) require water-resistant stencils, while solvent-based print mediums (gutta) require solvent-resistant stencils. You must also supply them with a

OBLONG SCARF. © Sally Jones. *This is another example of Sally's rich designs. The coffee cup motif adds a feeling of whimsy to this oblong scarf.*

photographic positive of your design; this means that you simply execute the design in black on white paper. Ask the photo screen supplier what kind of original image you will need to supply.

There is a thermal screen process that is similar to the photo screen process but it is simpler and faster. The process uses a polyester screen fabric coated with a heat-sensitive plastic film emulsion. A screen stencil is made by first copying your design on white paper using a copier with carbon-based toner. To make the stencil, place the copied image face up against the smooth emulsion side of the screen, exposing it to an intense flash of light (heat).

A Thermal Fax can be used to make the stencil from your design. The screen fabric is available in 9" x 12" sheets or by the yard for water-based and solvent-based print mediums. Fabric and screens for water-based dyes, and new or reconditioned Thermal Fax can be ordered from Welsh Products, Inc. (see List of Suppliers).

PRINT MEDIUMS

There are a number of methods for screen printing a design on silk. When using print mediums in conjunction with the other silk painting processes in this book, you should run tests to make sure that all the processes are compatible. A mixture of dye and a print paste can be screened directly onto the silk through the screen. Another technique is to screen a water or

solvent-based resist onto the silk and then dye paint.

You can also experiment with mixtures of print paste and dye-discharging agents made for silk (no chlorine bleach). When the discharge paste is screen printed onto silk that has already been painted and steam set, the agent will remove the dye color, creating a lighter design on the fabric.

Print Pastes and Preparation

Both acid and fiber-reactive dyes can be thickened for use as print mediums in the screen printing technique. Sodium alginate (available from fibric art suppliers) is a nontoxic thickener made from seaweed. Gum tragacanth is another thickener that works well with the chemistry of acid dyes. Both are packaged in a granular form and expand and thicken when mixed with water. The dyes are added once the print paste has been prepared.

Sodium alginates are of either the low-viscosity or high-viscosity type. Low-viscosity alginate is better for screen printing on silk because it consists of smaller particles, which can be squeegeed through a fine mesh for delicate line definition.

Sodium alginate itself does not sustain bacteria and will not grow mold, but the addition of water when making the print paste may promote bacterial growth. When a sodium alginate print paste ages, it will become thinner but may still be usable; just make sure it is not so thin that it seeps under the stencil during printing. To prolong its shelf life and retard spoilage, refrigerate the sodium alginate paste and, if you want, add a food

OBLONG SCARF. © Sally Jones. *Once Sally has completed her fabrics, she coordinates the patterns into panels for scarves. Each scarf is double-sided, and many of her luxurious scarves also have double-sided borders.*

preservative to it. When stored properly, the print paste should last up to three months. Always allow the paste to reach room temperature before using.

Print pastes that are to be made with liquid dyes should be mixed thicker than the pastes made with powdered dyes. The reason is that you must compensate for the additional liquid of the dye. When mixing a print paste with powdered fiber-reactive dyes, you will need to add a manufacture-recommended chemical water to the paste mixture to help the dye bond with the silk before and during the steam-fixing process. For the most part, prepackaged liquid acid dyes do not require auxiliary chemicals for steam-fixing and can therefore be added to an alginate paste that is made only with water.

Powdered acid dyes, on the other hand, are not traditionally packaged with acid and so you must add white vinegar (which contains 5 percent acetic acid) to the paste mixture to lower the pH level to approximately 4. This will ensure the fixing and full richness of the colors. You should test the pH level of the paste prior to adding the dye, and you can do this with testing materials available through chemical suppliers.

To prepare approximately one quart of print paste, you will need four cups of liquid, which will vary in composition, as specified here, according to which type of dye you plan to use. Note: When working with powdered dyes, wear a mask and rubber gloves for protection.

Recipe for Low-Viscosity Sodium Alginate Paste

(yield: approximately 1 quart)

4 cups of the appropriate liquid as follows:

> *Prepackaged liquid acid dyes:* 4 cups warm water, or slightly less if more concentrated color is desired

> *Powdered acid dyes:* 1 tablespoon white vinegar plus enough warm water to equal a total of 4 cups

> *Powdered fiber-reactive dyes:* 4 cups of the appropriate chemical water (chemical water instructions supplied by the dye manufacture or supplier)

3¾ teaspoons metaphos (the active ingredient in Calgon)

For *liquid (acid) dyes:* 5 tablespoons sodium alginate LV

For *powdered dyes:* 4–5 tablespoons sodium alginate LV

Mix as instructed on the following page and let sit for a minimum of 15 minutes in the storage container (or overnight for a smoother consistency). Note that metaphos is the pure form of sodium hexametaphosphate, which is also in Calgon. Metaphos is preferable, but Calgon is more common and may be easier to find.

You will also need the following equipment:

- a blender or large plastic, glass, or stainless steel mixing bowl, and a spoon
- measuring spoons and cups (glass, stainless steel, or plastic)
- 2-quart plastic storage containers for the paste

Mixing the ingredients. Pour the four cups of warm water into the blender and add the metaphos. With the blender on a low speed, slowly add the sodium alginate. Once the surface is no longer pulled under by the blending (about two minutes), pour the paste into the plastic container.

If you are mixing the print paste by hand, rather than using a blender, you may need another person to help you. Pour the four cups of warm water and the metaphos into the large bowl. One person sprinkles the sodium alginate very slowly into the warm water, while the other rapidly stirs the mixture.

Checking the print paste consistency. When working with powdered dyes, check the consistency of the print paste before adding the dye. For liquid dyes, check the paste consistency after adding the dye.

To check consistency, spoon up a large scoop of print paste and let it drip off the spoon. The print paste should flow in a steady stream. If the paste is too thick, it will break and not flow easily or evenly. To thin it out before adding powdered dyes, add a bit more water. To thin it out when using liquid dyes, add more liquid dye. When adding ingredients, add only a little at a time and test frequently. The paste should be slightly thicker than honey.

Adding dye to the print paste. It is easier to mix a deep, rich color from the concentrated powders than it is from liquid dyes, which are really intended for painting directly on the silk. When making a print paste out of liquid dyes, take care that the mixture does not become too thin. One way to compensate for this is to prepare a thicker print paste by adding less water to the alginate.

Acid dye powders should first be made into a slight paste with a small amount of boiling or very hot water. Slowly add more boiling water until the powder is completely dissolved. The mixture should be allowed to cool to room temperature and then added to the print paste. For a medium shade, start with ½ teaspoon of dye to 1 tablespoon water per 4 cups of print paste. You may find that a few powdered acid-dye colors are difficult to dissolve. Try adding a little bit of urea to the cooled solution to help dissolve any stubborn dyes. Urea is a powdered solubilizing agent available through chemical suppliers. It will decompose at high temperatures, so don't add it to boiling or very hot water.

Test your shades by smearing the colored print paste on a scrap of silk. When adding highly acidic colors to the print paste, the pH level may become too low, causing the alginate to break down and curdle. On the rare occasion that this happens, add an acid donor (ammonium sulfate or ammonium oxalate salts available through chemical suppliers) to the print paste to increase the acid content. It won't change the chemistry of the dye but will prevent the acid from reacting with the alginate.

When dissolving powdered fiber-reactive dyes, the optimum temperature for the mixture depends upon which type of dye is being used. MX-range fiber-reactive dyes need 75- to 95-degree water, while H-range dyes can withstand hotter temperatures. Neither should be dissolved in boiling water.

Gutta Resist

Clear gutta can be used as a treatment on both unpainted and painted grounds. Screening the gutta treatment onto the silk

THE AVIARY (detail). © Jane Herzenberg Design Studio. *Early in her professional career, Jane produced a collection of designs by screen printing her gutta resist. Here you see an example of a linear resist motif that was printed over a light yellow ground and then painted.*

THUNDER MOUNTAIN SWAMP. © Kerr Grabowski. Photo by Sean W. Hennessy. *Kerr started building this design by using leftover yardage from a previous project. She painted directly over this fabric with fiber-reactive dyes and created the highlights with Presist, which was applied to select areas to discharge the color.*

through a paper stencil design creates a lot of interesting possibilities. After it is applied, dyes will move and flow easily on the untreated areas of the fabric, but will not flow when painted on the treated parts. On these treated areas, you will be able to paint clearly-defined brushstrokes and create shapes that will not disperse on the silk.

The sticky gutta must be thinned with Turpenoid or mineral spirits so that it can be pulled through the open mesh with the squeegee. You will need to experiment to find a printable consistency that still maintains a good resist. Start with a mixture of 80 percent gutta to 20 percent solvent, and, if necessary, thin it down a 60:40 ratio. The gutta will be runny and difficult to control in a narrow screen well. A wider 2½- to 3-inch well may prevent the liquid from overflowing onto the silk. Depending on the weight of the silk, you may need to pull the gutta across the screen twice to penetrate its fibers. The fumes from the gutta treatment are strong so work in a well-ventilated area. Whenever possible, let the prints dry outside.

To clean, place the screen on a stack of newspapers. Wear rubber gloves and rub the screen with a soft rag saturated with Turpenoid or mineral spirits. Change the paper as it absorbs the gutta and solvent. The solvent is highly flammable so exercise caution when using it. Do not store solvent-soaked materials in your studio; let them dry outdoors.

Water-Based and Water-Soluble Resists

H. Dupont has developed a water-based screen printing resist for production art called Serti HPNO. It is an acrylic-like substance and is hard and permanent once it dries on the silk. Since it cannot be washed or dry-cleaned out and has a stiff texture, its use should be limited to open linear patterns (rather than solid, dense shapes) in order to preserve the soft drape of the fabric. Despite this limitation, it does have some unique features. It can be screened in a linear design over a painted ground and tinted with dye to impart a colored resist line.

Inkodye and Presist are other water-soluble resists that offer successful screening results when working with both acid and fiber-reactive dyes. If using acid dyes, do not use alcohol diluent; water-based resists are not as durable as gutta and wax and will break down easily when used with alcohol. The water-soluble resists are screened onto silk (similar to gutta resist), and both wash out in warm water after steam-fixing. As with all water-based resists, the Presist will discharge (partially remove) the previously unfixed ground colors over which it is printed, leaving a hint of any underlying color. Once the resist is applied, the silk is steam-set and the resist is removed, taking with it some of the underlying unset color. This characteristic creates subtle highlights when painted or screened onto already painted silk. Inkodye will also discharge color but not as much as Presist.

DEMONSTRATION:
Screen Printing with Gutta Treatment

In the following demonstration, I use the Moyer Design Fabric Stretching System to illustrate screen printing and gutta resist treatment techniques. This is the general procedure for screen printing, which you can adapt to any print medium. Just keep in mind that you must prepare your screen appropriately to accommodate either water- or solvent-based print mediums.

To prepare a ground to screen, I have stretched the silk on the Moyer Design frame, which is raised above the work surface on its removable legs. For the ground seen here, I first applied a wash of alcohol diluent to the fabric to achieve softer brushstrokes and deter the dye from striking the silk. Then I painted the design using a combination of wet and dry brush techniques and let it dry thoroughly. Other painting techniques that can be used to decorate printing grounds are: ombré (the gradual blending of one color into another), line building (using the line edges formed by dye washes to create designs), and salt. Gutta treatment printed on white silk can also result in some exciting possibilities.

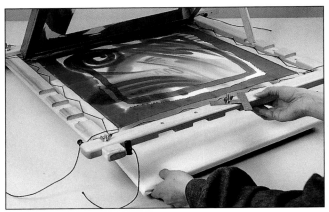

After the silk has dried, I remove the frame legs from the stretcher, attach the screen and hinge bar over the frame, and place the print board underneath. To hold the screen in position while printing, I use a flat T-plate (like those used for industrial bracing) and a ¼-inch machine screw (1 inch long). For protection, the sharp corners of the T-plate have been covered with duct tape. To prop up the screen (as in the next picture), you can attach a thin piece of wood to the side of the screen.

Here I arrange a paper stencil made from freezer paper cut-outs on the fabric, coated side facing up toward the screen.

You should always lower the print frame at this point to check the position of the stencil pieces. If satisfied, turn the T-Plate to secure the screen.

For this project, I used gutta treatment (thinned gutta) for the print medium. Pour the medium into the top screen well and pull it toward you to the bottom of the screen with the squeegee. You should use both hands for this, and hold the squeegee at about a 45-degree angle to the screen. The angle of the squeegee will determine the amount of print medium deposited on the silk: the larger the angle, the thinner the deposit; the smaller the angle, the thicker the deposit. To prevent drips on the screen after a pull, pull all the print medium entirely into the bottom well, and keep the squeegee off the mesh when not in use. It is best to only pull the ink over the screen once because repeat pulls may cause the stencil to shift, disturbing the print registration.

Immediately after printing, remove the stretcher frame with the printed fabric from the print board, reattach the legs (as in the following photograph), and allow the silk to dry. Also keep in mind that once one print has been pulled, the print medium will keep the paper stencil adhered to the screen, enabling you to pull a few additional prints. (Any fabric necessary for multiple printings must be stretched and prepared for printing beforehand.)

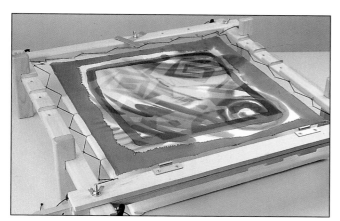

Once you have completed the printing, use a rubber spatula to scrape off any unused print medium. Save this for reuse. Remove the stencil and clean the screen thoroughly with the appropriate solvent.

Screen printed gutta treatment gives the silk painter some exciting creative options. Since the dye will move easily on the untreated areas (those that were covered by the stencil), these spots can be filled in with flowing color. Here I fill one untreated section with dye, which flows up to the edges of the treatment and then stops. Dye can also be painted on the areas of gutta treatment (the spots that were not covered by the stencil), but it will not move as it does on untreated areas. This is because the treatment controls the dye flow. Each brushstroke will remain visible and clearly defined, and the results will look similar to painting with watercolor on paper.

9 PRACTICAL CONSIDERATIONS

Once your silk painting or garment is complete, you are ready for the finishing process. Proper finishing techniques give your work integrity and the respect it deserves. Steam fixing and framing increases the presence of your artwork and imbues it with a finished quality that sets it off from its surroundings. It is very rewarding to see one of your compositions mounted and framed or to wear a beautiful handpainted silk scarf or tie. Your skill and creativity should be proudly showcased.

When finishing your work, you must consider both the time-tested methods and the materials used so that you can best extend the life of these creations. Setting the dyes in the fabric properly and framing and caring for the silks in a way that promotes longevity will ensure lasting enjoyment.

MURAL IN THE ELEPHANT BAR AT THE EAST 21 HOTEL IN TOKYO (details).
© Antoinette von Grone

STEAM FIXING

Not only does the steaming process set the dye permanently and bond it with the silk, it also develops the color to bring out all its brightness and intensity. Once the dyes are fixed, your silk creations can be washed or dry-cleaned. (Note that silks containing metallic gutta and some pigmented resists should not be dry-cleaned; follow instructions on product packaging.) During steaming, heat and moisture penetrate the silk to create a concentrated dye bath, which sets the dye. Pébéo Soie, Tinfix Design, H. Dupont, and Jacquard Red Label Silk Color dyes all require steam fixing. (The Jacquard Green Label Silk Colors are immersed in a premixed dye setting solution.) Steaming will also remove some of the wax resist used in the painting processes. Any residue of clear gutta and wax still remaining in the silk will be removed when the silk is dry-cleaned. After dry cleaning, the silk is rinsed to remove any excess dye and chemicals.

Steaming equipment can be purchased, or simple household items can be used to assemble a steamer, like the canning pot used in the following demonstration. A large stove pipe steamer can also be assembled for steaming yardage by using large galvanized stovepipe or double walled stainless pipe (which can be purchased at a local plumbing and heating supplier) placed in a heavyweight cooking pot (or an electric pan) filled with a few inches of water. The layers of paper, cloth, and silk (as discussed below) are rolled around a wire mesh or paper tube and then suspended in the pipe above the water. To absorb condensation, a cover of newspapers and towels are used to seal off the top.

Preparing the Silk

Before steaming, the painted fabric is first wrapped in newsprint or in cloth (for example, old poly cotton sheets) and then rolled in a covering of kraft paper. (Moving supply companies are a good source for inexpensive packing newsprint paper that can be purchased by the pound. Left over ends of newsprint rolls can also be purchased from your local newspaper printer.) All the paper used for steaming should be uncoated and porous so that steam can penetrate through the roll to reach the silk during the fixing process. (See the demo for rolling instructions.)

Paper is fine for silks with resists such as clear gutta and wax that are to be dry-cleaned out of the fabric later. The paper also absorbs some of the wax resist so if there is only a light coat of wax, you can eliminate the need to iron the wax out prior to steaming. However, cloth is more appropriate for wrapping silks containing decorative resists that will remain in the fabric (black or metallic gutta). Paper has a tendency to tear and stick to a tacky resist, and this will ruin your artwork. Cloth, on the other hand, can be pulled free of the resists more easily than paper, and the cloth can be washed and reused.

Steaming

Since steaming paper emits potentially toxic fumes, the process should be done outside or near a strong exhaust fan. Depending on the thickness of your rolled silk, the weight of your fabric, and concentration of dye, the dye-painted silk should remain in the steamer for 2 to 3 hours. For wearable art, 3 to 5 hours is recommended. Include a sample piece of silk that contains the colors and resists you used in your art in the steaming so that you can test the success. You will need to check the water level periodically and refill the steaming pot with water if necessary.

To do this, use a large funnel so you can direct the water into the bottom of the steamer. Do not let the steamer boil dry or your silk will discolor or, even worse, turn to ashes. Once you have completed the process of steaming, you will be better able to gauge the times when you will need to add water as well as the amount of time it takes for a successful steaming.

When the steaming time is up and the heat is turned off, immediately remove the package from the steamer. Take out the sample piece and test to see if your steaming was successful by submerging it in water. If you see clouds of color coming off the silk into the water you will need to steam your artwork longer. If the steaming was successful, unroll it, and allow the silk to air dry. If the kraft paper is not damaged, it can be reused and the cloth should be washed before it is used in another steaming.

Storing the Steaming Pot

Once a pot has been used for steam fixing, consider it a fabric steaming pot that should not be used for food preparation. After completing the steaming process, remove the canning rack and save the circular newspaper padding (see demonstration). Clean the pot, and let the damp padding and assembled lid (towel and padding) air dry so they can be reused. Once dry, the rack and padding can be stored in the clean steaming pot.

DRY CLEANING

After the silk has been steamed, it should be dry-cleaned to remove any remaining gutta or wax. Dry cleaning is a textile-cleaning process that uses solvents instead of water. There are a variety of solvents that can be used; common ones are benzene, naphtha, and perchloroethylene, a solvent often used by professional dry cleaners. Dry cleaning solvents require special handling and, oftentimes, permits for their use and disposal. So, while you could dry-clean your work yourself, it is probably best to keep personal health and environmental awareness in mind and use a professional dry-cleaning service. There are bulk dry-cleaning businesses, often located in local laundromats, which charge by the pound or load. Even if your silks weigh much less than the maximum weight per load (which is usually approximately 8 to 10 pounds), bulk dry cleaning will still be more economical than dry cleaning per piece.

RINSING, IRONING, AND CLEANING

Once the dyes have been steam-fixed and the silk dry-cleaned, the fabric should be rinsed in water to remove any excess dye, chemicals, or salt residue, and restore the natural pH level. For optimum bonding of the dye to the fabric fibers, wait 48 hours after steam fixing before rinsing the silk. Rinse it in a tub of luke-warm water (70 to 90°F). (Professional silk painters often add Synthrapol to the rinse to remove loose dye and deter backstaining.) Use plenty of water so that it can circulate completely around the silk and wear rubber gloves to protect your skin from the chemicals. Do not twist or wring the silk, and do not let dark areas touch light areas for any length of time. Repeat this rinse process two to three times. To neutralize any traces of alkali, the next to last rinse should include white vinegar (use one tablespoon per quart of water).

To remove the excess dye and the chemicals that can potentially damage the silk over time, the silks that do not require dry cleaning should also be rinsed as above. This will also restore

DEMONSTRATION: Steam Fixing

To prepare the package of rolled silk and paper (or cloth), lay a large sheet of kraft paper on a clean, flat surface. Place 2 to 3 layers of newsprint paper or cloth on top of the kraft paper. Place your fabric on top of these layers, leaving a 2-inch border of newsprint on all sides, and cover with 2 to 3 more layers of newsprint or cloth. Before and during rolling, smooth out the fabric so that wrinkles do not occur during steaming. To protect your fabric from condensation, the kraft paper should extend beyond the ends of the newsprint enough so that the rolled layers of silk and newsprint are enclosed in 3 to 5 layers of kraft paper.

If you are steaming more than one layer of silk, place 2 to 3 layers of paper or cloth between each layer of painted fabric, ending with a layer of paper or cloth on top. Pieces of painted silk fabric can be put next to one another, but they should not overlap. Roll the layers together, and as you do this, smooth out any creases in the fabric. Keep the ends of the roll even, and tape the roll securely.

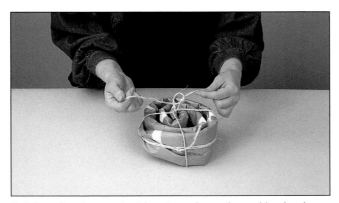

Coil the roll and secure it with string or heavy-duty rubber bands.

Use a canning pot for the steamer. To assemble it, first pad the lid. Cut a pile of newspaper (⅜- to ½-inch thick) into a circle that fits inside the lid. Lay the paper on a thick cotton towel, and place the lid over it. Gather the sides of the towel up and fasten tightly and securely over the top of the lid.

Invert the canning rack and place it in the bottom of the pot. Fill the pot with approximately 1 to 2 inches of water. The water level should be at least 2 inches below the top of the rack so that the boiling water doesn't splash onto the rolled package. To further protect the package from any splashes or condensation, place 1 circular sheet of aluminum foil on the rack and then place more circular layers of newspaper (⅜- to ½-inch thick) on top. Once the water is boiling, position the silk package on the paper-padded rack. To avoid condensation damaging and spotting your silk, check that both the package and newspaper pad are not touching the sides of the pot. Also make sure that the padded lid clears the top of the package.

To prevent a fire, give the towel a final inspection to ensure that it will not hang or slip over the sides of the pot. Once the water is boiling and the lid is on the pot, adjust the heat source so that it maintains an even, constant simmer and periodically add more water.

the silk's natural softness and pliancy. Repeat the rinsing process described above until the water runs fairly clear, and again do not twist or wring the fabric, or leave in a heap.

After rinsing, roll the silk in a clean towel to remove excess water and hang (or lay flat on top of a towel) to dry. You can iron the fabric while still damp to better remove wrinkles. Ironing silk while it's damp gives it a pleasantly soft hand and also increases the richness of the colors. Redampen if necessary. Set the iron on the synthetics/steam setting. Place a press cloth or tissue paper on top of the silk to prevent leaving iron marks on your designs and always iron on the wrong side. Black and metallic guttas will smear on the silk and iron so always put tissue paper over and underneath the fabric while ironing. Replace the tissue paper as soon as it becomes soiled so that it does not restain the silk.

For general washing of soiled silks, hand wash in lukewarm water with a mild soap like Ivory Liquid or Liquid Tide. Never use harsh detergents or bleach. Most garments constructed out of painted silks, which have been properly steam-set and rinsed, are hand-washable, but delicate, highly constructed garments should be dry-cleaned to maintain their shape.

FRAMING ARTWORK EXECUTED ON SILK

Framing is an art form in and of itself. It requires superb aesthetic judgment and craftsmanship. The function of a frame is to protect and visually separate a piece of art from its surroundings; but it shouldn't be so noticeable that it distracts from the artwork. The frame should highlight and encourage the viewer to focus on your silk painting. The quality of the framing job conveys an artist's professional integrity and respect for his work and audience. The type of frame selected is a reflection of personal taste and style, and can even be the result of a collaboration between the artist and the client.

Professional framers often use a mat (a border around the artwork) as an additional means of setting the artwork off from its surroundings. When mounting artwork under glass, the mat (usually a heavy cardboard) also prevents the silk from coming into contact with the glass (or clear Plexiglas—acrylic plastic sheets) and any condensation (from the air) that might collect on its underside. The mat can also be integrated with the design, becoming part of the artwork itself. For example, sometimes artists Linda and David Hartge cover their mats with painted silk. The pattern of the mat silk complements the patterns in the artwork. However, whatever style you choose, frame and art should form a cohesive unit.

Protecting Silk Under Glass

Paintings are often framed behind glass to protect them from dirt, dust, and grease (from cooking and fingerprints). The backs of the frames are sealed with a backing board or paper. Since part of the beauty of silk painting is the tactile quality of the fabric, many artists find it difficult to put their work behind glass. They lament that a layer of glass physically and psychologically separates the viewer from the work, preventing intimate contact with the sensual qualities of the textile.

If, after careful consideration, you decide the artwork should be behind glass, there are a few options available to you. Conservation nonglare glass, or a clear acrylic-like Plexiglas or

Should I Use Glass?

To help you decide whether or not to use glass, consider these practical issues:

- As a rule, silk paintings should be kept out of direct sunlight. Heat and sun destroy silk fibers and fade dyes. Ask yourself to what environmental elements the painting will be exposed, other than direct sunlight; glass may help protect against excessive moisture and dirt. Also keep in mind the projected life span of the artwork; glass may help extend it.

- Where will the painting be hung? Will it be displayed in a gallery, shop, art show, office building, restaurant, or private home? If the artwork is to hang in a restaurant, glass will help protect it from harsh elements such as smoke and grease. If the piece is intended for a less-trafficked bedroom, one might be less inclined to use glass so that the sensual qualities of the fabric can be fully appreciated and experienced.

styrene, filters out ultraviolet rays and cuts down on reflection and glare. Dyes will be protected from both ultraviolet and indirect sunlight, which may also cause colors to fade. Sheets of acrylic are not as fragile or as heavy as glass, making them an excellent alternative when framing artwork that will travel. However, acrylic does scratch easily and should be cleaned with a nonabrasive cloth and clear spray wax or soapy water. Do *not* use traditional cleansers or glass cleaners, which will cause the acrylic to cloud or become foggy.

Unlike many other materials, silk is a natural fiber and needs to breathe. Therefore, when mounting silk under glass, make sure that air is still able to circulate around the fabric. One way to ensure proper ventilation is to punch a few small holes in the backing paper before taping it to the frame. Professional framers use a hole punch to keep the holes neat.

Planning for Successful Artwork

Before beginning a silk painting, you will need to consider the characteristics of your chosen fabrics. Determine which stretching technique will be most suitable for your silk and will ensure that the finished work can be properly mounted and framed. Plan ahead; if you do not, you may end up with unsatisfactory results. It may take a little experimentation and a few compromises before you find the compatible materials and techniques that work best for you.

Many silk painters prefer to work with crepe fabric because, unlike habutai, it can be stapled (to a frame) without developing pulls and runs. Also, the resilient and flexible quality of the crepe weave enables it to adjust for stress points on the frame over which it will be stretched and tacked down. These stress points, which tend to develop and become more apparent over time, are more visible in the plain, woven fabrics. They are also less noticeable on crepes because this silk is not as shiny as other varieties and, therefore, is less likely to reflect any stress spots.

Stretching Techniques

Traditionally, tapestries and delicate fabrics were stretched and mounted by being laced around a board or some other flat sur-

MENDOCINO. © Natashe Foucault. *This painting has been wrap-stretched over wooden stretcher bars.*

Planning Tips

- *Design.* Consider your design in relation to your framing technique. For example, an image with a straight-edged border painted on a stretchy fabric will be difficult to stretch for framing. If you are not careful as you stretch the fabric, the border may also stretch unevenly. To prevent this and make the stretching job easier, make sure that any straight border lines in your design follow the grain of the fabric so that they are not pulled out of shape. Another alternative is to avoid painting straight borders on your composition. Many interesting borders make use of abstract shapes and wavy lines.

- *Measurements.* Fabrics can shrink in length up to 2 inches per yard during the steaming, dry-cleaning, and rinsing processes. If you are not prewashing your fabric, you may want to factor in extra length when measuring the silk for a project. Also, add a 2-inch border around a painting for ease in handling and tacking down the silk during the stretching process.

- *Stretcher bars.* Lightweight canvas stretcher bars are an inexpensive support for displaying silk paintings. The painting is stretched over and wrapped around this wooden support frame, as in the demonstration later in this chapter. Also called wrap-stretching, this solution eliminates the need for a frame. If you are planning to use the wrap-stretch technique, you must increase the planned dimensions of your design by about 2 inches so that the silk can be wrapped around the back of the frame without distorting the image.

Cliffs of Kitayamazaki. © Vello Lannemaa. Photo by artist. *Source of inspiration photo by Tositaka Morita 1984.*

CROCUSES. © 2002 Kai Vaarandi. Photo by Vello Lannemaa.

(ABOVE) NECKWEAR. © 2002 Vello Laanemaa. Photo by Tiit Rammul, set up by artist. *Commission from DaimlerChrysler AG for an International Seminar in Tallinn, Estonia.*

(RIGHT) NECKWEAR. © 2001 Kai Vaarandi. *Both Kai and Vello use the Pebeo Setasilk brand of iron-set flowing paints to produce the rich colors and subtle blending found in their work. To blend color on the silk when working with iron-set flowing paints, Vello and Kai recommend keeping your fabric wet, only allowing it to dry after achieving your desired effect. They also recommend that you dilute Setasilk with water because the diluted paint does not change the hand of the silk, and a small amount goes a long way.*

face. But double-sided acid-free tape, the staple gun and archival dry mount glue paper have made contemporary stretching and framing projects much easier. Some artists stretch and staple their paintings over an acid-free foamcore board, which is first covers with a layer of thin, white polyester batting. This technique is suitable for both heavyweight and delicate, lightweight silks.

Other artists use double-sided acid-free tape to mount their paintings on acid-free foamcore. To use, measure and cut tape to desired length and adhere one side of it onto the foamcore. Then remove the shiny protective paper covering to expose the adhesive on the other side. You can now position and adhere the fabric on the tape. For larger paintings, you might also want to reinforce the tape by stapling the silk through it onto the foamcore at 1-inch intervals.

Artist Sybil Shane works with an archival dry mount glue paper and mounts her paintings to be framed on archival white mat board or heavy white cotton rag paper. The glue paper can be purchased in sheets up to 40″ x 60″ and by the roll. To accommodate the size of a painting, she sometimes uses two pieces of glue paper. Being careful not to overlap the edges, she simply butts the edges together. Sybil cuts the glue paper ⅛″ smaller than the edges of her silk painting. She then adheres the silk to her surface by ironing from the center out.

Artist Suzanne Punch stretches her large, abstract paintings executed on medium- to heavyweight crepe de chine over lightweight canvas stretcher bar frames that have first been covered with a stretched piece of white cotton flannel. The flannel gives the silk body and helps protect the delicate fabric from the bare wooden stretcher bars. It also prevents the bars from shadowing or showing through thinner silks. Once a painting is stretched, there is a wide selection of manufactured frames that will fit around canvas stretcher bars. Suzanne slips her paintings into simple, precut, metal sectional frames without mats or glass.

A note of caution: I have spoken to silk painters who, on the advice of professional framers, have had their work professionally laminated with heat-sensitive adhesives to foamcore or acid-free board for framing. After several years or a sudden change in humidity and temperature, bubbles have formed under the silk. This is partially due to the natural expanding and contracting of the fabric. Some lamination and mounting processes may be permanent, so the fabric cannot be removed for cleaning and then reattached. Keep this in mind if you choose a mounting technique like this.

STRETCHING SILK OVER CANVAS STRETCHER BARS

In the following demonstration, I stretched a painting over lightweight canvas stretcher bars like those mentioned previously. The dyes in your artwork should be set, and the silk should be thoroughly washed. The fabric doesn't necessarily need to be ironed, though, because the stretching process will pull it smooth. The stretcher bars must be unwarped, so check this before you purchase them. If your bars are longer than 44 inches, you should reinforce the frame with a crossbar.

If you are planning to frame your painting after it is stretched, select a frame that is made with a deep enough rabbet (groove) to accommodate the depth of the stretcher bars, and any glass, mat, and backing board you might be using.

JELLIES. © 2001 Elizabeth Heber. *Liz's inspiration comes from the Sea Nettles in the fabulously lighted display tanks found at the Monterey Aquarium. Her spirited drawings captures the moment and her color is spontaneous, giving each jelly and painting a life of it's own. Liz works with Tinfix Design, Dupont dye, clear gutta and Dupont decorative resists.*

Materials

4 lightweight canvas stretcher bars

4 right-angle corner clamps

right angle

polyurethane and brush

glue (make sure it will work on wood)

sandpaper

¾-inch acid-free framer's tape

double-sided, acid-fee adhesive tape

white cotton flannel (washed and rinsed well)

ruler and tape measure

mat knife

scissors

staple gun and fine, rustproof staples with a ¼-inch tack point (depth)

staple remover

small hammer

4 to 8 pushpins

dressmaker's marking pencil

clean water in a spray bottle

kraft paper

hair drier

picture hanger

DEMONSTRATION: Stretching Your Silk Painting

In this wrap-stretch method for displaying a painting that will not be framed, the artwork is stapled to the back of the stretcher bar frame. For work that is to be framed, the painting is stapled to the sides of the stretcher bar frame, and the excess fabric is trimmed off.

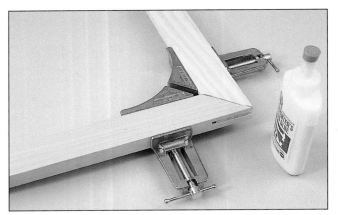

A day or so before you plan to stretch your silk, prepare the stretcher bar frame by sealing the wood with a coat of polyurethane. This will keep the chemically-treated wood from discoloring and eroding the fabric. Let the bars dry thoroughly and then set the frame in corner clamps. Use the right angle to establish a 90-degree angle at each corner. One corner at a time, release the clamp, glue the bars together with wood glue, and reclamp. Double-check your angles, and let the glue dry thoroughly. Remove the clamps, and sand the corners and edges to eliminate any rough spots or bumps that might catch the silk or distort the painting's surface.

Stretch your artwork (right side down) tautly on a clean work surface and tack the edges down with four strips of acid-free framer's tape or masking tape. Position the stretcher frame over the fabric. Using a dressmaker's pencil, put a mark on the center of the inner side of each bar and place corresponding marks on the back of the artwork. Also mark the placement of the frame's corners on the back of the silk. Measure the depth of the stretcher bar frame (in this case, ⅝ inch) and add ⅛ inch to that. Draw a border on the fabric around the frame at a distance from the bars that is equal to this measurement (here, ¾ inch). (For artwork that is to be stapled to the stretcher bar sides, not the back, draw a line next to the frame.) As in the photograph, apply strips of ¾-inch acid-free framer's tape to this line, stopping 2 inches in from each corner. (The tape will prevent the staples from creating pulls in the fabric, and will later act as a guide for stretching and positioning the silk on the frame.) Now remove the tape that is holding the silk to the work surface. The silk may ripple a bit; this is to be expected.

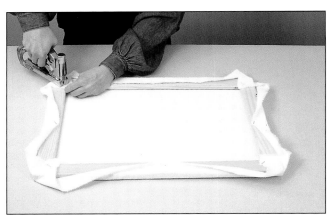

Cut a piece of flannel to cover the frame. Each side should equal the corresponding bar length plus an extra 4 inches. Stretch the flannel onto the frame, and, using a staple gun, place one staple through the fabric in the center of each bar. Also put a temporary staple through the fabric in each corner.

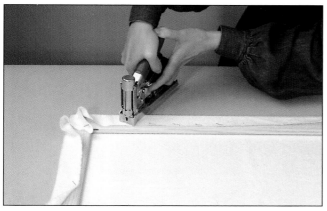

Staple each side from the center to within 3 inches of each corner. Do one side and then its opposite. While doing this tacking, keep the grain of the fabric straight, and place the staples at a slight angle to avoid weakening the fabric.

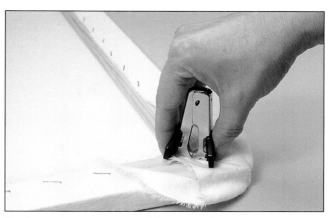

Use the staple remover to carefully remove the temporary corner staples.

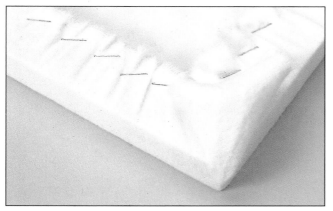

Pull and stretch the fabric away from the corners, easing the fabric into soft gathers. Smooth out any wrinkles in the flannel on the sides of the frame. If the wrinkles are stubborn, remove a few staples and rework the fabric until the flannel lies flat against the frame, and restaple. Smooth, neat corners are very important, especially in an unframed wrap-stretch.

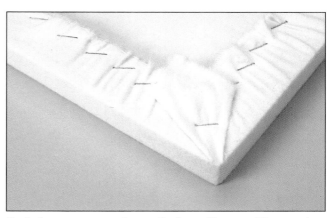

Staple the corners securely over the frame. Use a small hammer to lightly tap any protruding staples into the wood.

Using the positioning marks drawn earlier, place the flannel-covered frame onto the back of the artwork. Stretch the silk onto the back of the bars so that the tape is approximately ⅛- to ¼-inch in from the inside edge of the frame. (Note that the acid-free tape is not removed. It is under the silk so you don't see it.) Press the silk into place. Secure with one pushpin in the center of each side.

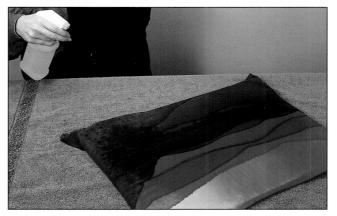

Flip the painting over and dampen the front with water. Make sure you keep the water away from any tape. Keeping the silk damp, stretch and staple the painting exactly as you did the flannel. The staples should be placed through both the silk and the underlying tape at a slight angle. Use the tape as your guide, and work from the center of each bar to within 3 inches of each corner.

Pull and stretch the corner fabric until it is smooth. You may need to carefully remove and restaple a few spots. At this point, you should hang the painting for a few days to be sure that no sagging or unevenness develops. If it does, remove a few more staples and readjust the silk. Again, lightly tap any protruding staples into the wood. (If you have stapled the silk to the sides of the stretcher frame and if the painting is to be framed with glass and backing materials, you may need to trim off any excess fabric that is creating too much bulk for the rabbet.)

To back a wrap-stretched painting, cut a piece of heavy kraft paper that is approximately ⅛ inch smaller (all around) than the framed piece. Adhere it to the back of the frame with double-sided tape.

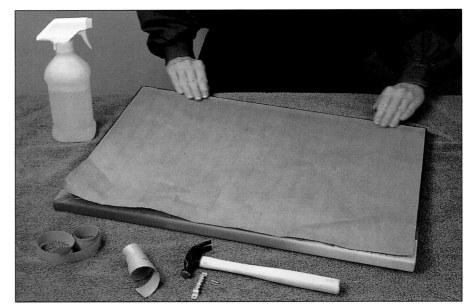

For a more professional-looking framing job, wet the backing paper by evenly misting or sponging it with water.

Dry the backing paper thoroughly using a hair drier. As the paper dries and becomes taut, push down on the strip of tape so that the paper does not pull loose.

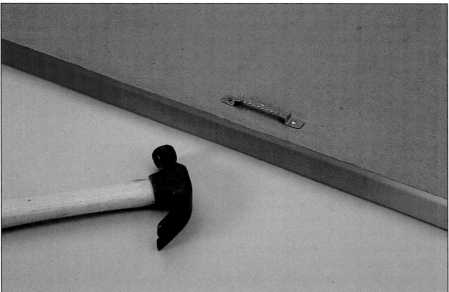

To attach the picture hanger, find the center on the back of the top bar of the painting. (The one pictured here is an adjustable Moore sawtooth picture hanger.) Place the hanger near the lower edge of the bar, making sure that it is parallel to the top edge, and lightly mark this placement with pencil. Hammer the nails (that come with the hanger) through the hanger into the back of the stretcher bar frame.

The stretched, wrapped painting is ready to be hung.

LIST OF SUPPLIERS

Aljo Manufacturing Co.
81-83 Franklin Street
New York, NY 10013
(866) 293-8913
(212) 226-2878
FAX (212) 274-9616
www.aljodye.com
sales@aljodye.com
powdered acid and fiber-reactive
dyes and related chemicals

• **Atelier de Paris**
1543 S. Robertson Boulevard
Los Angeles, CA 90035
(310) 553-6636
FAX (310) 553-9621
www.atelierdeparis.com
rosemary@atelierdeparis.com
importers of H.Dupont dyes
and related products, manufac-
ture of Rocco products, silk,
steaming service, workshops

Dharma Trading Co.
P.O. Box 150916
San Rafael, CA 94915
(800) 542-5227
(415) 456-7657
FAX (415) 456-8747
www.dharmatrading.com
inf@dharmatrading.com
H. Dupont, Tinfix Design, Pébéo,
Jacquard dyes and related products, fiber reactive dyes, silk

• **Exotic Silk**
1959 Leghorn
Mountain View, CA 94043
(415) 965-7760
(800) 845-SILK outside CA
(800) 345-SILK in CA
FAX (415) 965-0712
www.exoticsilks.com
info@exoticsilks.com
silk by the yard, scarf blanks

G&S Dye and Accessories Ltd.
250 Dundas St. W, Unit 8
Toronto, Ontario M5T 2Z5
Canada
(800) 596-0550
FAX (416) 596-0493
www.gsdye.com
info@gsdye.com
Pebeo Soie, Setacolor, related
products, silk, workshops

Galerie Smend
Mainzer Strasse 31
50678 Cologne, Germany
(0221) 31 20 47
FAX (0221) 9 32 51 34
www.smend.de
smend@smend.de
Tinfix Design, H. Dupont dyes
and related products, German
books on silk painting, silk,
workshops

John Marshall:
Works in Fabric
The Old Flour Mill
PO Box 115
(76302 Main Street)
Covelo, CA 95428
FAX/PHONE (707) 983-6636
www.JohnMarshall.to
katazome@johnmarshall.to
Japanese brushes, shinshi,
books, workshops, soy sizing
(gojiru) info

Maiwa Handprints
6-1666 Johnston Street
Vancouver, B.C.
Granville Island,Vancouver,
BC V6H 3S2, Canada
(604) 669-3939
FAX (604) 669-0609
www.maiwa.com
maiwa@maiwa.com
Pébéo Soie, Setasilk and fiber-
reactive dyes and related
products, print screens,
print powders, silk, shinshi,
Japanese brushes, workshops

• **Moyer Design &**
Silk Painting
Susan Louise Moyer
PO Box 2875
Fort Bragg, CA 95437-2875
(800) 780-6377
FAX (707) 964-7677
www.moyerdesign.com
susanlouise@
         moyerdesign.com
Moyer Design Fabric Stretching
System™, dyes, dye sets and
related products, brushes, brush
sets, books, fabric steamers,
private lessons, international
workshops

Personalized Embellishments
3697 Bell Road
Nanaimo, BC, V9R 6X3
Canada
TOLL FREE (877) 353-2211
FAX (250) 758-5701
www.fabricprintingfx.com
millerkarene@shaw.ca
heavy duty freezer paper for
backing silk

• **PRO Chemical & Dye, Inc.**
P.O. Box 14
Somerset, MA 02726
(508) 676-3838
(800) 2-Buy-Dye
FAX (508) 676-3980
www.prochemical.com
pro-chemical@att.net
Pébéo Soie and fiber-reactive
dyes and related product, print
paste materials and all related
chemicals, workshops

• **Qualin International, Inc.**
P.O. Box 31145
San Francisco, CA 94131
(415) 970-8888
FAX (415) 282-8789
www.qualinsilk.com
qualinint@aol.com
H.Dupont, Tinfix Design, and
related products, silk by the
yard, scarf blanks, yarn, ribbon

• **Rupert, Gibbon and**
Spider, Inc.
P.O. Box 425
Healdsburg, CA 95448
(800) 442-0455
FAX (707) 433-4906
www.jacquardproducts.com
jacquard@sonic.net
wholesale/retail
Jacquard products, books,
steamers, silk fabric

• **Savoir Faire**
40 Leveroni Court
Novato, CA 94949
(800) 332-4660
FAX (800) 299-3113
www.savoir-faire.com
info@savoir-faire.com
importers of Tinfix Design dyes,
Isabey brushes and related

products, will provide list of
retail store

• **Silkpaint Corporation**
P.O. Box 18
18220 Waldron Drive
Waldron, MO 64092
(800) 563-0074
FAX (816) 891-7775
www.silkpaint.co
art@silkpaint.com
H. Dupont dyes and related
products, Silkpaint Air Pen

• **Thai Silks**
252 State Street
Los Altos, CA 94022
(415) 948-8611
(800) 722-SILK outside CA
(800) 221-SILK in CA
FAX (415) 948-3426
www.thaisilks.com
thaisilks@thaisilks.com
silk by the yard, scarf blanks

Uline:
Shipping Supply Specialists
(800) 295-5510
heavy duty freezer paper
product #7047

• **Welsh Products, Inc.**
(707) 745-3252
(800) 745-3255
FAX: (707) 745-0330
www.welshproducts.com
wpi@welshproducts.com
full line of thermal screen
products

• **Wolfmark Neckwear**
101 W Edison Avenue
Appleton, WI 54915
(920) 954-9895
(800) 621-3435
FAX (920) 954-6802
www.wolfmarkties.com
www.americanmadeties.com
sales@wolfmarkties.com
makes ties, scarves, and hats
from your painted silk yardage;
call for pattern layout before
painting

• ACKNOWLEDGEMENT: A special thank you to the suppliers for their support in the business of publishing this revised edition of *Silk Painting for Fashion & Fine Art.*

OTHER RESOURCES

ASSOCIATIONS

American Craft Council (ACC)
SUBSCRIPTIONS (888) 313-5527
PROFESSIONAL MEMBERSHIP (800) 724-0859
www.craftcouncil.org
council@craftcouncil.org

Silk Painting International (SPIN)
www.silkpainters.org
phil@pkldesigns.com

Studio Art Quilt Associates (SAQA)
(514) 937-8061 FAX (541) 937-8061
www.saqa.com
info@saqa.com

Surface Design Association (SDA)
MEMBERSHIP (707) 829-3110
FAX (707) 829-3285
www.surfacedesign.org
surfacedesign@mail.com

MAGAZINES

American Craft
published by the American Craft Council
SUBSCRIPTIONS (888) 313-5527
PROFESSIONAL MEMBERSHIP (800) 724-0859
www.craftcouncil.org
amcraft@craftcouncil.org

American Quilter
SUBSCRIPTIONS (270) 898-7903
FAX (270) 898-8890
www.AQSquilt.com
AQSquilt@apex.net

Belle Armoire
SUBSCRIPTIONS (949) 380-7318
(877) STAMPER (782-6737)
FAX (949)-380-9355
www.bellearmorie.com
belcustomerservice@stampington.com

Fiberarts
(829) 253-0467 FAX: (828) 253-7952
subscriptions@fiberartsmagazine.com
www.fiberartsmagazine.com

Ornament
SUBSCRIPTIONS (800) 888-8950
ornament@cts.com

Quilting Arts Magazine
SUBSCRIPTIONS (866) 698-6989
www.quiltingarts.com
info@quiltingarts.com

Surface Design Journal
published by the Surface Design Association
SUBSCRIPTIONS (707) 829-3110
FAX (707) 829-3285
www.surfacedesign.org
surfacedesign@mail.com

Threads
SUBSCRIPTIONS (800) 888-8286
FAX (203) 426-7184
www.threadsmagazine.com
th@taunton.com

INTERNET GROUPS

www.yahoo.com
  groups
      silkpainting
      silkpainting@yahoogroups.com

      waxeloquent1
      waxeloquent1@yahoogroups.com

      complexcloth
      complexcloth@yahoogroups.com

Additional resources and updated information can be found under Links on Susan Louise Moyer's website: www.moyerdesign.com.

HIDDEN VALLEY © Karen Rosen and Carole Mondress of Kalalani Silk Painting Studio.

ORCHIDS IN THE MIST © Karen Rosen and Carole Mondress of Kalalani Silk Painting Studio.
In Hawaiian, Kalalani means heavenly colors. Karen and Carole chose Kalalani for their name and have been designing and painting together in Hawaii since they formed their partnership in 1988. For years these creative entrepreneurs have often worked simultaneously on the same painting. Through this collaboration they have learned to trust each other and surrender to the flow of their process, creating a fertile environment that nurtures their individual points of view, artistic expression, and professional growth. Working together and with the Jacquard Green Label Colors, Karen and Carole have captured the beauty and powerful radiant light of the Hawaiian Islands.

INDEX

POPPIES. © Linda France Hartge and David Hartge. *In this painting, two images from nature are used as contrasting elements. The poppy plant naturally creates strong upward movement that is enhanced by the vertical format of the composition. The diagonal lines created by the bending iris leaves contrast this motion, while the bold primary colors (also found in nature) add life and drama to the work.*